LEFTWARD HO!

The American Institute for Progressive Democracy
(TAIPD)
a 501(c) 3 non-profit educational organization.

Engaging Thought and Promoting Action

TAIPD is committed to strengthening and extending democracy, social justice, economic well-being and peace for all peoples, within the context of environmental and economic sustainability. We do so with the belief that the quality of life, in all of its aspects, can be improved for the vast majority of Americans and for the other peoples of the world. We envision a collaborative society that seeks to build a community in which individuals accept responsibility for the well-being of all.

www.taipd.org
www.taipdconference.com
www.facebook.com/taipdorg

Other Books from The American Institute for Progressive Democracy

Pithy Progressive Polemics – edited by Merrill Ring
The Impact of Israel's Founding Myths on the Prospects for a Two-State Solution – Andrew J. Winnick

LEFTWARD HO!

Political Ideas and Criticism from
Progressive Democracy
2011 – 2014

Corrected Edition

Edited by Merrill Ring

Progressive Democracy is the online journal of
The American Institute for
Progressive Democracy

ISBN-13 978-1544867632
ISBN-10 1544867638

First edition 2016
Corrected Edition 2017

Preface

The American Institute for Progressive Democracy began its online journal *Progressive Democracy* in 2011. The aim was to publish pieces of various kinds written from a distinctly leftish (progressive, social democratic, liberal) point of view. The aim for the articles was not to track day-to-day or month-to-month political developments, but to step back a modest way from those attention grabbing events (and commentaries on them) in order to write about the *ideas* embedded in them. Further, the aim was to write for an intelligent but non-academic audience.

A writer for the journal then had to satisfy two criteria: divorcing oneself (though not too far) from the events of the day and writing to be readable by an intelligent audience.

Looking back on the essays published in *Progressive Democracy*, those aims have been pretty well satisfied.

In fact, as I re-read everything we have published I have been struck by how thoughtful those writings are, how almost all have managed to find the middle ground between too closely connected to current events and too distant. And because of that almost all still are capable of speaking to a reader of today. It was that continuing relevance that justifies the publication of the best of those pieces in book form. As articles they have otherwise vanished into the journal's archives, but they are still fresh and interesting and worth reading as pieces of progressive political thinking and writing. (A few have been omitted because they were a little too out of date.)

The largest omissions belong to a different category. Not every interesting thought people have come in chunks of (say) 750 words. In fact, some of the very best parts of longer essays are a paragraph or so, material that could stand on its own feet. So under the heading Pithy Polemics we publish in each issue short and memorable pieces. Those pieces for the years 2011-2014 have already been published in book form: *Pithy Progressive Polemics* is available at Amazon books.

The items published here are also from the year 2011-2014. The reader will find them still relevant, even striking, as expressions of progressive thought, pieces of various lengths on a wide range of topics.

All proceeds from ales of this book will go to the Institute – the authors themselves are satisfied that they have made a contribution to the progressive tradition.

MR
December 2016

Corrected Edition
I simply made too many proof-reading mistakes in my haste to get this published in 2016. Hence this corrected edition.

MR
February 2017

Contributors

Charles Bayer has been a pastor and theological professor in the United States and Australia. He and Wendy live at Pilgrim Place Claremont, CA. He currently serves on two not-for-profit boards, writes a weekly widely circulated political column, and is a watercolor artist. He is also a former member of a Claremont City committee dealing with hate crimes and hate incidents.

Tad Beckman is Emeritus Professor of Philosophy at Harvey Mudd College. With a background in both chemistry and philosophy and a developed involvement in Native American studies, he has recently published five books as Kindle eBooks. He maintains a blog at tadbeckmans.blogspot.com concerning current politics and political philosophy.

David Depew taught philosophy at California State University, Fullerton and, until his recent retirement, rhetorical studies at the University of Iowa.

Bob Gerecke retired from Los Angeles County service as Principal Welfare Fiscal Analyst. His last assignment had been as staff for 5 years to the Citizens' Economy and Efficiency Commission. Having been an active investor since the 1960's, after retirement he worked for 6 years in the financial industry as a stockbroker with an insurance license. a founding member of the Institute's Board. He is a founding member of the Institute's Board.

John Grula has a PhD in biology with very wide interests. For nearly 20 years he has been Astronomy Librarian at the Carnegie Observatories in Pasadena. He writes a column for the Pasadena Weekly on the intersection of science and public policy. He is affiliated with the Southern California Federation of Scientists.

Ivan Light is a Professor of Sociology (Emeritus) at UCLA and is a founding member of The American Institute for Progressive Democracy. He is past President of the International Migration section of the American Sociological Association, a recipient of that group's career achievement award, and the author of five books about immigration. He has recently published a novel about the sinking of the Lusitania (*Deadly Secret of the Lusitania*), recounting the British and American propaganda about that sinking which helped cause our entry into the disastrous World War I.

Merrill Ring is Professor of Philosophy (Emeritus) at California State University, Fullerton – he is a member of The American Institute for Progressive Democracy board and is the editor of *Progressive Democracy*. He has edited the volume *Pithy Progressive Polemics*: *Political Ideas and Criticism from Progressive Democracy 2011-2014* – available on Amazon books in both paperback and Kindle editions.

Chris Rubel once acquired a PhD in Pastoral Psychology and has been many things in his life: an Episcopal priest, a therapist and a truck-driver. Now retired, he describes himself as an Appreciator.

Stephen Simon has taught and written philosophy, edited museum publications, visited and written about Palestine, cut sugar cane in Cuba – the article here is the result of a recent visit to Cuba.

Andy Winnick is Professor of Economics and Statistics, California State University Los Angeles. He is the President of the American Institute for Progressive Democracy. His most recent book is *The Impact of Israel's Founding Myths on the Prospects for a Two-State Solution* available in both paperback and Kindle at Amazon books.

David Winnick holds a MBA in International Business & Management from Thunderbird, The Graduate School of Global Management. He works and lives in Germany, and is active in progressive politics there.

CONTENTS

LEFTWARD HO!

Cuba: A Modest Proposal (Issue #14)

By Stephen Simon

Simon's suggestion as to how start normalizing relations with Cuba is an imaginative way to break free of the status quo by making an end-run (as you will see, that is to mix sports metaphors).

In 1962 President John F. Kennedy issued an executive directive to place Cuba under an embargo. This was part of several pieces of Cold War machinations involving Cuba that resulted in the shifting of Cuba's economic relations from the "West" (primarily the US) to the "East" (Soviet Union and Warsaw Pact Countries). From that time until 1991 Cuba became deeply dependent for exports, imports and foreign aid on the East. What the US lost, the Soviet Union gained: a dependent state.

All this ended with the collapse of the Soviet Union in 1991, the breaking free of Eastern European countries from the Soviet Union and their moving into the spheres of the West: NATO & the European Union. For Cuba, this was devastating. It lost its Soviet patrons and its Eastern European markets. In the attempts of Eastern European countries to gain acceptance by the West and especially to gain entrance into NATO and the European Union, they then became partners in the American embargo of Cuba.

1991 began what Cubans call "The Special Period" or "The Special Period of Austerity." These were truly grim times. Because of the increased power of the American imposed embargo, Cuba found itself very hard pressed to acquire capital goods or export its agricultural goods. Soon, its monetary reserves depleted, it could purchase very little of even "humanitarian goods". Superstructure began eroding and a national policy of rationing was put into place simply to ensure that people had a bare minimum of nutrition in order to survive.

One can easily imagine that at this point some semi-enlightened US administration could have said, "Look, we have won the cold war. There is no longer a Soviet menace 90 miles from our shores. Let us sit down with the Cubans and work out some compensation arrangement for business losses, etc."

But, of course, that didn't happen. Instead, something truly monstrous happened. In order to gain the support of Florida and assure his victory in the 1996 presidential election, Bill Clinton signed the Helms-Burton Bill. This not only widened the embargo against Cuba, but also turned it into law. It meant, of course, that ending the embargo was no longer a matter of presidential action. As things stand today, it takes an act of Congress: a two-thirds majority in each branch of Congress. You cannot get two-thirds of the members of Congress to agree that the Pope is Catholic.

What to do? Here is a modest proposal for a start. Instead of tilting directly with Congress, instead of trying to selectively poke holes in the embargo, or enlarging exceptions, suppose we tried to initiate some new relationships between the people of Cuba and the U.S.

What about a couple of major league Cuban baseball teams being invited to play in the major leagues? There are already Canadian teams in the big leagues – why not go 90 miles south too? Cubans think of themselves as North Americans. Guess what? Cuba isn't a soccer country. Baseball is the Cuban national sport! There are even some Cubans who think that Cubans INVENTED baseball. And there are outstanding Cuban teams.

Inviting one or two Cuban teams to play in the major leagues (rather than having individual Cubans defect in order to play there) could be a first step in laying foundations for normalizing relationships and eventually ending the embargo.

It would at least throw a fastball past the Cuban-American community in Miami!

Capitalism (Issue # 22)

By Tad Beckman

Capitalists and Conservative defenders of capitalism assume a form of capitalism in which there is no moral burden on Capitalists, no moral responsibility for the well being of those in the community who join in the productive process by selling their labor.

The Conservative Right likes to see themselves as the guardians of Capitalism. Liberals, in the worst light, are viewed as Socialists at the very least and, when tempers get really riled up, Communists. The trouble with the Conservative right's position is that they neither define nor justify the particular form of Capitalism which they are guarding. However, Capitalism can have many forms depending on the character of the people involved.

In the most basic sense, Capitalism is simply an economic system in which there is private ownership of the means of production. At the time of our nation's founding, the economy was agrarian so the principal means of production were land and tools involved in farming the land. The majority of Capitalists were independent farmers, the very population upon which Jefferson rested his utopian concept of a democratic government. With so much in common, people would be able to come together to participate in government and solve their shared problems.

Of course, even in the infancy of our nation, there were already economic factors that, as they developed, would topple such a utopia. There was already an industrial-agricultural split between New England and the South. And Southern Capitalism depended upon slavery. In the North, the means of production were moving toward the tools and institutions of industry and away from mere land and cottage tools.

In the era of industrial production, Capitalism took on an entirely different appearance. Since the means of production were becoming factories and large-investment machines, Capitalists were far fewer in number and the remainder of the population increasingly turned to laboring for their means of survival. As Marx saw it, Capitalist society became increasingly divided between the Bourgeoisie (Capital owning class) and the Proletariat (laboring class).

The notion of "means of survival" is interesting in the context of this discussion. In a strictly agrarian society the "means of production" are equivalent to the "means of survival". That equivalence continues for the Capitalist in an industrial society, but the remainder of the population is alienated from the means of production so that its survival becomes contingent. Capital is a means of survival for the majority of people only in the contingency that they are able to sell their labor at a price that can sustain them.

Today, the vast majority of Americans depend on selling their labor in order to survive. While 80% of Americans were still small farmers in the late 19th century, the percentage of small farmers now is so small that the U.S. Census has dropped the category as inconsequential. But selling our labor depends entirely upon the management of Capital and that means an enormous division of power.

Jeffersonian democracy is a thing of the past. No matter how one wishes to characterize the American government today, it is no longer a coming together of equals to solve shared problems. It is far more an "oligarchy in democratic clothing".

In fact, the system of industrial Capitalism places an enormous moral burden on a small number of people since the welfare and survival of the majority of their countrymen has become their responsibility. That is the sad truth – sad because with only a few exceptions Capitalists have largely ignored this burden.

The situation is rather like that of the doctor Plato describes whose true role is nurturing the health of patients, but who becomes so involved in the making of money that his patients' health suffers.

Capitalists of the late 19th century enhanced their profits by buying labor at the lowest possible price, one established by the most meager sense of survival: the simple ability to get up the next day and work again. Anyone injured in the process or becoming ill or refusing the indignity could easily be replaced. So long as the aim of the Capitalist is simply maximizing profits all kinds of terrible things can happen.

I see no problem with the Capitalist system of economy if the moral burden is understood. That burden is to produce products of superior quality for delivery to consumers and to contribute to the well-being and survival of the people who contribute to production by selling their labor.

But this burden requires that Capitalists focus on other matters than pure profit taking. The quality of products is a simple matter of honesty. Caring for the well-being of those who work for you is a less simple but still clear matter. The means of production are useless without the help of those who labor: hence, the welfare of those who labor is an obligation that must be met. It is not a matter of simply buying labor at the minimum wage possible: it is a mater of functioning as part of a cooperative community.

This piece was originally published on Tad Beckman's blog: www.tadbeckmans.blogspot.com

Small vs. Big Government (Issue #6)

By Bob Gerecke

When was the last time you heard a liberal say 'We want big government'? The framing of the issue by the right as Small vs Big is picked up and repeated by the media without it ever being asked whether that is the progressive message. This piece sets the record straight.

We shouldn't be seeking either small or big government, but government that does what we need it to do -- whatever that may be. In some cases we may add to what government does, in other cases subtract. Each case should be decided on its own merits. We the people, acting through our government, shouldn't refuse to do something just because we're doing other things, nor should we use our government to do something which duplicates or supplants what our other social institutions are doing satisfactorily. In addition, we should ask whether something which the government has been doing is still needed or can be improved, and whether we can utilize government to improve upon something which businesses and nonprofits aren't doing as well as is needed. We must do that case by case.

That being said, the increasing complexity of society and of human affairs and the increasing power of technology often require us to use government to do more. A simple and concrete example is regulation of vehicles and their use. When automobiles were first invented, the roads weren't paved. When roads were first paved, there were no lines dividing the lanes, no stop signs or traffic lights, and no rules of the road. Eventually we needed all of these things. As vehicles became faster and accidents more dangerous to life and limb, we also wanted to improve the safety of the vehicles themselves. As we filled the air with smog, we began efforts to reduce emissions. Changing the roads and the rules could only be done through government. Changing the vehicles could be done by producers acting on their own, but if costs would be incurred, it was sometimes necessary to establish a requirement upon all producers or an agreement with them in order to maintain a level playing field, overcome the disincentive of cost, and make an impact. And all of the rules needed enforcement.

We can't go back to an earlier and simpler age in this case and in many other cases. We can just try to create effective and efficient laws, regulations and enforcement mechanisms to the extent any are needed. That's not easy work, and it often requires correcting mistakes.

There have been arguments over cost-benefit analysis. It's appropriate, but sometimes it has been conducted inaccurately, by ignoring indirect costs or by considering only financial costs. But the principle is correct: we should maximize benefits and minimize costs.

Small-government advocates sometimes describe money paid to the government in taxes or fees as money taken away from the private economy. That's not true, because government spends what it receives, usually as quickly as it receives it, and it spends most of it here in the USA. Unlike multinational businesses and affluent individuals, it doesn't invest much of it outside of the country (our foreign aid is around 1% of the Federal budget) except during wartime. The money paid to public employees, contractors and suppliers in the USA enters our own economy the moment it's paid.

Some small-government advocates argue that government can't do anything right. Both government and our other institutions make mistakes, but government's mistakes are usually public knowledge, whereas the mistakes of businesses and nonprofits are often unknown to outsiders or at least not publicized by the news media. We also have a higher standard for government than we have for other institutions. We expect government to get it "right"; we expect other institutions only to equal or outperform their competitors. For example, we don't say that auto manufacturers can't get it right because their vehicles haven't always had turn signals, extra brake lights in the rear windows, seat belts and air bags, or because they've had recalls and keep redesigning their products, or because they don't meet every customer's desires. We don't castigate every vehicle that isn't perfect, but we do that when considering government policies and programs.

The Soviet Union is usually held up as the example of how badly everything is run when the government is in charge. However, it wasn't comparable to government in a democracy. The Soviet government was a dictatorship, not responsive to the people. Better examples of the role of effective government in providing both regulation and services can be found in the Scandinavian countries, which have blended the best of capitalism and socialism.

Whereas government agencies (and corporations which possess monopoly or at least dominance, according to management literature) tend to err by being too resistant to change, many businesses tend to err by incurring too many risks to themselves and to others or by sub-optimizing (seeking to maximize their own gain at the expense of others, or their short-term gain at the expense of the future). In some cases caution is more effective, in some cases risk-taking is. That becomes part of the analysis of which institution is better for us to use in a particular case.

Government's main weaknesses in deciding (at the policy level) what to do and how to do it are two-fold:

1. Elected officials are too afraid to annoy the special interests which raise or can raise

substantial sums of money to help or hinder re-election, even when those interests make demands which are contrary to the wider public interest.

2. Elected officials and government bureaucrats don't look ahead; instead they react to public or special interest demands here and now.

The first problem can be remedied by major campaign finance reform. That will help to remedy the second problem as well, because it will free officials to be less reactive to special interest demands and will increase the election of officials who have wisdom and integrity.

Some states have effective models of campaign finance reform. They have avoided court rejection because they don't prevent fund-raising from private sources; instead they provide competitive public financing for candidates who reject private fund-raising. Public financing of candidates for State office doesn't directly affect elections to Federal office, but it does affect the pipeline of State office-holders who move up to run for Federal office. And it may be legal to publicly finance even Federal candidates, as long as it doesn't conflict with Federal laws and regulations for those who opt to remain in the private fund-raising arena. Meanwhile, the Internet is providing an alternative source of publicity and funds for candidates who don't have sponsorship from the well-heeled special interests. If this grows enough, it may provide some degree of reform in addition to any government action.

Corporations' main weaknesses in policy-making stem from the disconnect between their executives' compensation and the companies' long-term health. Salary, bonuses and stock options are tied too much to short-term results. Because corporate CEO's select their own boards of directors, and because these boards consist of other CEO's or people who report to other CEO's, compensation decisions are rigged to maximize CEO rewards regardless of how things turn out in the long run. The gross size of these rewards ensures that a CEO will be wealthy even if forced to resign after a short tenure because of incompetence. The lack of input from customers and employees in the decision-making process, and the obstacles to election of alternative directors, further ensure that the corporation is a dictatorship of, by and for the CEO. Until corporate governance is reformed, corporations will continue to operate in a sociopathic manner, i.e., without regard to the wellbeing of others.

Nonprofits' weaknesses vary from incompetent or self-aggrandizing board members to ineffective or domineering administrators. They do best when attacking a narrow issue or problem but have difficulty with multi-faceted missions, and if financially successful they often become institutionalized, i.e., more interested in the size and wealth of the institution than in the achievement of its supposed mission. It even happens to religious institutions.

No organization is perfect – governmental, business or nonprofit. Politicians and commentators can improve the intellectual and practical level of the debate by avoiding grand philosophical arguments and slogans over big vs. small government and instead arguing over the merits of specific cases.

The Boston Tea Party: Lessons for Today
(Issue #20)

By Merrill Ring

What was the Boston Tea Party all about? What we did not learn as children and why it is applicable to our problems today?

I'm going to start with a story, one that we all know. It is a story about an event that led to the Declaration of Independence and to the Independence Day we are celebrating today. It is the story of a tea party – the original one, the Boston Tea Party.

As we all know, a hundred or so Bostonians, disguised as Indian warriors, boarded three ships in Boston harbor, ships loaded with cargoes of tea. They proceeded to smash open the tea chests with their hatchets and dump the tea into Boston harbor. About 90,000 pounds of tea went into that particular drink, enough tea to make about 24 million cups, tea worth in today's dollars $1.5 to $3 million dollars.

13

That is what we as school children in this country have all learned. However, in those same history lessons there is something we were not told, were not taught to think about. Whose tea was it that was tossed into the water? That matter has not become part of American consciousness, though it should be.

It certainly wasn't American tea: that much our orthodox histories are clear about.

But the answer standardly guessed at, and in fact encouraged by those with a particular political axe to grind, is mistaken. It was not government tea either – it was not British government property although the normal telling of the story suggests that it was.

The tea the tea partiers destroyed belonged to a corporation – to the East India Company.

The East India Company was the biggest corporation of its time – sort of the Exxon Mobil of its day. In 1773 corporations were fairly new public entities – there weren't yet many of them. But there was the East India Company and it was big and powerful.

What we need to incorporate into our historical consciousness today is that our famous Boston Tea Party was an attack on a major corporation and involved the destruction of a large amount of corporate property. Let's retain our belief that the raiders were American heroes but realize that they were heroic in taking direct action against a massive corporation.

To further develop our understanding of America's history we today need to ask, and to teach our children to ask, a further question.

Why did a handful of angry American colonists engage in an attack on a corporation, an attack which succeeded in their intention of destroying corporate property and which has become a symbol of American resistance?

The Boston Tea Party came about because the East India Company had acquired a monopoly on the importation of tea into the colonies.

Americans were a tea drinking country in the 18th century.

Prior to the East India Company's acquiring the sole right to provide tea to the Americans, our ancestors had their tea supplied either by Dutch traders or by American shipping entrepreneurs. The East India Company had seen to it that it became a crime to bring tea into the colonies either by Dutch or American ships: East India Company ships became the only legitimate transporters of tea into the colonies.

To make matters worse, in 1773 the corporation had vast quantities of tea in its warehouses in Britain and needed to unload it (a practice we today call 'dumping' though not the dumping the tea party patriots employed.) So it had convinced the British government, which of course ruled the colonies, not to charge taxes on sales in the colonies of that excess tea. The East India Company could thereby undercut the price of any remaining illegal tea smuggled into the colonies.

In short, they had a stranglehold on the tea supply for Americans.

We, who are re-learning this piece of American history, must now ask: how had the East India Company acquired that monopoly? How did they convince the British government that they shouldn't have to pay taxes on their business activities?

The answer is simple and sad: all (or nearly all) members of Parliament owned stock in the East India Company – even the King, good old mad George III, was a stockholder.

Since the corporation stood to make more money by having the sole right to provide tea to the colonists and since most members of the British government, even to the very top, were stockholders in the company and thus, as individuals, stood to gain financially from granting the corporation that monopoly and tax break, there was no question what the government would do: corporate power and the ability to enrich oneself prevailed.

So much for the history lesson. It is time to move on to today.

Thomas Jefferson wrote that there were three roadblocks to freedom in the young country that we were: government, organized religion and monopolies – the name he used for corporations, for large and powerful business organizations such as the East India Company.

Organized religion has faded – but not vanished – as an impediment to democracy and people power in this country.

So we individuals, private citizens, today confront two massive domestic centers of power: our various governments and the hugely increased number of giant corporations that dominate our economic system.

Worries about the extent of power exerted by those two different Jeffersonian roadblocks are what shapes American political thinking today.

We liberals/progressives/social democrats – by whatever name we are known and know ourselves – are suspicious of both sources of power over our lives.

However, and this is what distinguishes liberalism today, we also think that corporations are the largest source of uncontrolled and thus dangerous power in this country.

On the other hand, conservatives, especially including the group that wants to appropriate the name of the 1773 Tea Party, totally ignore the power of corporations in our lives. They focus solely upon the intrusiveness, actual and fanciful, of governments.

Why do we liberals think that corporate power is the biggest danger to the ideals of the United States and to the freedom and well-being of its citizens? The reason is clear: we citizens have virtually no control over corporations, whereas we citizens do have some degree and means of control over our governments – and we can have more if we are willing to work for it. As a democracy we can elect the people who run the government – we cannot do that for officials of corporations. Corporations, in the American system, are private entities, bodies not answerable to society. Further, they seek not the general welfare but their own advantage.

The best we in America can do – and it can be effective – is to produce laws and regulations to limit the power of corporations and the damage they do in the pursuit of their own private good.

Sadly, things are worse than I've so far made out – for we haven't yet touched on the lesson of the Boston Tea Party and the East India Company. The even larger danger is that through their wealth and consequent power, corporations can subordinate governments, the other major source of power in today's America.

That is, they can buy, directly or indirectly, the government just as the East India Company did. And they can thereby use it to pursue their own ends rather than the good of the country and its citizens, again just as the East India Company did.

Liberals today see this country returning to the same cozy arrangements that led to the Boston Tea Party. Corporations and corporate wealth and power are increasingly buying our government. This country is shifting from having a modest control of corporate power – control that was chiefly a legacy of Franklin Delano Roosevelt – to a country where the effective governing power is that of gigantic business organizations.

Our Revolutionary War was fought to free ourselves from a government that was in the pocket of a corporation. That form of business organization has proliferated and we are increasingly governed by corporate power and money. It is time to take control of corporations – to have a 21st century Boston Tea Party, a new Declaration of Independence.

Current tea baggers, who presume to think of themselves as heirs of the real tea party, fail to see that their own activities and thoughts are paid for and at the mercy of today's corporations. They are thus of no help at all in solving the major problem besetting our democratic politics.

Jefferson again: "I hope that we shall crush in its birth the aristocracy of our moneyed corporations, which dare already to challenge our government to a trial of strength, and bid defiance to the laws of our country."

We did not do it then – it is time to do it now.

And a good Independence Day to you.

An earlier version of this was given as a 4th of July speech at the Speaker's Corner during the 2013 Independence Day celebrations in Claremont, California.

Examining The Tea Party Movement: An Old American Tradition, A New Phenomenon
(Issue #2)

By Andy Winnick

A thorough account of the history and nature of the Tea Party.

When one talks about the Tea Party Movement, it is

essential to recognize that there are three separate layers or elements of this new political phenomenon which has emerged since 2008-2009. However, before examining this structure, it is important to understand the origins of the movement.

The History of Political Populism and Libertarianism in America

Obviously, the term "Tea Party" is a reference to the pre-revolutionary Boston Tea Party in 1773 in which American colonials boarded British ships and threw bundles of tea overboard to protest the tea taxes imposed by the British government.

More significantly, it is important to understand that, from the dawn of American history, government and the dominant political parties, with great regularity, have had to deal with the "intrusion" of populist movements seeking to "confront the establishment" and the major political parties. This strong cultural current is deeply embedded in the American psyche. Many argue that it flows directly from the legends and mythologies, as well as from the facts, surrounding the American Revolution. Many Americans simply feel entitled to challenge established social and political forces.

Certainly, the writers of the U.S. Constitution were well aware of this current, and, one could argue, were deeply afraid of it. This is seen in such aspects of the U.S. Constitution as the fact that senators were to be chosen, not by direct election of the people of a state, but by state legislatures, and that the President and Vice President were not to be elected by direct election of the people, but by members of an Electoral College chosen by the states (which is how G. W. Bush became president even though Al Gore received hundreds of thousands more votes). It is also relevant that initially the right to vote was not only withheld from slaves, "Indians" and women, but was also denied to white males who did not own property. Farm or industrial workers who did not own "real" property (a house, a farm), could not vote. This anti-democratic current is also seen in the fact that American elections are always held on Tuesday workdays, not weekends. One can well argue that the intent of all the barriers placed between the common people and political power was to prevent the "rabble" from having a direct influence on government.

But in response to these structures and to the constant presence of various elite groups, so-called "people's parties", populist parties and movements, have sprung up regularly in American history. One of the earliest was the Whiskey Rebellion (about a tax on liquor) in 1790, during the presidency of George Washington. In 1890, there emerged the People's Party based primarily on poor, white cotton farmers in the South and Texas and wheat farmers in Kansas and Nebraska. In 1912, Theodore Roosevelt split from the Republican Party, and led the Progressive Party in the presidential election, and Progressive Party candidates also ran in 21 governor's and 200 Congressional races. Few won, but the movement continued to run candidates until 1918 when it rejoined the Republican Party. Other populist movements/parties occur with great regularity in American history, including the Vietnam Anti-War Movement within the Democratic Party in the 1960's, about which more will be said below. Many focused on regional issues, while some assumed a national presence. Some formed into "Third Parties" to compete on a national basis against the established two major parties. Others constituted themselves as movements or factions within one of the established parties, seeking to bend that party to the will of the populist movement. In most cases, these third parties or movements were short-lived, typically dissipating within an election cycle or two.

Another strain of populism is the American libertarian movement. American libertarianism has its roots in the philosophy of the late-Enlightenment period and the term was first used in England in 1789. Political movements and philosophies that emerged in France in the 1880's and 1890's built upon this tradition. The modern American variant focuses on the commonly used words 'liberty' and 'freedom'. It argues that government is neither the grantor nor the protector of such rights, but is the primary violator of these rights. It views government "intrusion" into the lives of people and their businesses as the greatest danger to liberty and freedom. Efforts to levy taxes, regulate business, restrict the "right to bear arms" are all held to be expressions of this danger. So-called free-market libertarianism, an adherence to laissez-faire capitalism, is an integral part of this movement. Polls in 2006 indicated that about 15% of Americans considered themselves libertarians. The Libertarian Party was formed in 1971 and has run candidates in every presidential election since. It remains the third largest, formally structured political party in the U.S. When Republican President Ronald Reagan in the early 1980's said that "government was not the solution, government was the problem," and began referring to "the government" instead of to "our government," he was endorsing this belief, despite the fact that he was the head of government.

It was hardly a surprise that a number of people who were outspoken libertarians cloaked themselves in the mantle of the Tea Party Movement in 2010. The best known example was Rand Paul, who was elected to the U.S. Senate for Kentucky with Tea Party Movement support. His father, Ron Paul, has been a Congressman since 1976 and has the most conservative voting record of any member of Congress since 1937. In 1988, Ron Paul ran for president on the Libertarian party ticket, but in 2008, he ran in Republican presidential primary elections.

The Tea Party Movement is explicitly a self-described libertarian and populist movement. The essential thing to take away from this brief historical perspective is that the Tea Party Movement is quintessentially a traditional American phenomenon and is not at all an aberration.

The Structure of the Tea Party Movement–Three Levels

<u>Level One</u> - Most of the American public and the vast majority of the media restrict their attention to the public face of the Tea Party Movement. They see the large crowds rallying and demonstrating around the nation for different causes – to oppose the health care reform efforts of the Obama Administration, to support some candidate for public office, to pressure Congress to reduce government spending and the size of both federal and state government, to encourage free enterprise capitalism that does not have to suffer the interference of government regulation, to support state Governors who are trying to take collective bargaining rights away from public employees. These local groups are real, and exist now in every state in the U.S., though they are concentrated in the Midwest and South. One obviously cannot understand the Tea Party Movement without further studying these local groups, but first, let us identify the other levels of this movement.

<u>Level Two</u> - Above these local groups are five national organizations which work to coordinate and train local activists, help them to network and focus on national issues. These groups work by providing funds, convening conventions, sending out and training staff, and establishing communication networks.

These five groups are:

1. <u>The Tea Party Express</u>, led by Sal Russo and funded by the billionaire Koch brothers, with Sarah Palin and Michele Bachmann (Congresswoman from Minnesota) as spokespeople.

2. <u>The Tea Party Nation Corporation</u>, organized by Judson Phillips of Tennessee in 2009, which sponsored the National Tea   Party Convention   in February 2010, and which was reportedly able to pay Sarah Palin $100,000 to give the keynote speech.

3. <u>The Tea Party Patriots</u>, which is self-described as "a national grassroots organization that provides logistical, educational, networking and other types of support to over 1,000 community   based   tea   party groups." One report indicates that, in fact, it has more than 2,800 local affiliates.

4. <u>The National Tea Party Coalition</u>, which is apparently a loose linking of several dozen local Tea Party groups and which talks about encouraging "The Tea Party Ecosystem" of individuals and   local organizations   united   in   working   toward   "fiscal responsibility and limited government".

5. <u>The National Tea Party Federation</u>, which lists on its website 85 member and affiliate groups and which states that it was established to create a unified message and media response among   key   leadership and their affiliates.

There is a great deal of overlap among these organizations.

These five national groups give the Tea Party Movement a more national image and impact. For example, following President Obama's constitutionally mandated State of the Union address to Congress in February 2011, there was an official (and traditional, but not constitutionally mandated) response by

Republican Congressman Paul Ryan, chair of the House Budget Committee. But this year, there was also a response by Michele Bachmann that was self-described as the official Tea Party Movement's response. While every major TV network carried both Obama's address and that by Ryan, only CNN also carried the Bachmann response and labeled it as "official," despite the objections of some of their own commentators on-air. Bachmann and the Tea Party Express succeeded in giving their movement a moment of national impact.

Another example is the success of the Americans For Prosperity (AFP) group (discussed just below), and its leader, Tim Phillips, to organize, fund and bus into Madison, Wisconsin hundreds of Tea Party Movement activists from around Wisconsin and nearby states. The goal was to mount counter-demonstrations against trade union members and supporters, who were demonstrating to block a recently elected Tea Party governor who successfully stripped public employees of their collective bargaining rights. Without AFP money and organizing, this certainly would not have happened. The goal was to gain for the Tea Party Movement some portion of the vast attention the national media were giving to the Wisconsin situation – one of the first major, successful efforts to destroy unions since Ronald Reagan successfully decertified the air traffic controllers union in 1981.

Level Three – Standing above and behind these five national groups and the hundreds, maybe thousands of local organizations, there is a less visible and less talked-about group of extremely wealthy individuals and their very well-connected political operatives. It is these individuals and organizations who have created and funded the national Tea Party Movement structures and who manipulate and channel the efforts of the local groups, either via one or more of the five Level Two groups listed above, or by directly providing coordination, strategies and vast sums of money.

Most important among these are:

A. FreedomWorks, a split-off from a group established by the billionaire Koch brothers, David and Charles, was originally led by Dick Armey, Jack Kemp and C. Boyden Gray, all major Republican Party leaders.

B. FreedomWorks, still funded by the Koch brothers and led by Armey, runs training camps for Tea Party Movement activists and for those supporting candidates endorsed by that Movement. (It also supports some more establishment conservatives who have not gained, or maybe even sought, Tea Party endorsement.)

C. Americans for Prosperity (AFP) and its Foundation, both reportedly funded by the Koch brother's, claim to coordinate a network of "1.5 million citizen activists in all 50 states, with 31 state chapter organizations." Tim Phillips, president of both AFP and the AFP Foundation, claims to have received donations from "more than 80,000 Americans" and talks about "combining 'best- in-class' capabilities built at the national level with local knowledge from...on-the-ground armies (of Tea Party Movement activists)...." Tim Phillips apparently prides himself on being the best grassroots organizer in the U.S. today.

D.   American Crossroads and Crossroads-GPS were organized by Karl Rove (former Chief of Staff to President G. W. Bush) and Ed Gillespie (who is the former Republican Party Chairman). These groups have had to admit to spending tens of millions of dollars in support of the most conservative Tea Party Movement candidates in 2010 and are estimated to have spent $100's of millions. It is strongly suspected that they have also funded some of the Level Two national Tea Party organizations.

Together, these organizations help coordinate the political efforts of some of the most powerful corporations in the U.S. and represent the interests of many of the elite, wealthiest .01% of American families (which is less than 11,500 families, who control in excess of 5 times the wealth of the bottom 80% combined). Some of these wealthy individuals are quite activist themselves. These political operatives and wealthy individuals helped to organize, fund and even create some of the Level Two groups. They saw the potential political power in the spontaneous actions of the local, libertarian, populist groups as they reacted to what they had been told was true, especially about the health care reform effort (most of which was totally fabricated by the rightwing media). These operatives then channeled and focused these "grassroots" groups by providing money and coordination to co-opt their emotional and ideological concerns in order to gain support for issues identified by the operatives themselves as serving the interests of their corporate and elite clients.

There are, of course, other, better known and long established corporate groups, such as the National Chamber of Commerce and the Business Roundtable (an association of the CEOs of major U.S. corporations), that are also very politically active. The former apparently funneled more that $100 million in support of conservative candidates in the 2010 elections. However, these groups have not publicly linked themselves to the Tea Party Movement.

The Origins of the Term "Tea Party" Movement

The use of the term Tea Party Movement to describe the efforts that sprung up in 2009 by people opposed to the Obama Administration's health care reform effort, and Obama himself as President, was largely a creation of two media spokesmen: Rush Limbaugh, a rightwing radio commentator and Glenn Beck, a Fox TV news commentator. Some argue that the originator of the term was Sal Russo of the conservative political consulting firm Russo, March and Rogers, who founded the Tea Party Express group via the firm's political action committee, Our Country Deserves Better. The term 'Tea Party Express' was also applied by Russo to his touring bus of activists that traveled around the nation sponsoring anti-health care reform and anti-Obama rallies.

Other protest rallies occurred early in 2009 opposing the bank "bailout" effort (of the Bush Administration) and opposing the economic stimulus law signed by Obama within days of assuming office in February 2009. Some of those protestors dressed in colonial-style hats and coats and held signs talking about too much spending and taxes. Their garb may have given the cue to the media and Russo to employ the term 'Tea Party Movement'.

One of the symbols often adopted by populist movements in the U.S. is the Gadsden flag, a yellow field upon which is a coiled rattlesnake with a tail of 13 rattles, under which is written *Don't Tread On Me*. It was the first flag of the U.S. Marine Corps, carried by them in 1775 when they intercepted British ships carrying war supplies to aid the fight against the colonials. This flag appeared at many of the early 2009 rallies, and also suggested the colonial period and the revolutionary Tea Party theme.

Who Are the Tea Party Movement's Members and/or Supporters?

This is a difficult question to answer with precision. Since the movement is splintered into a variety of organizational structures, both national and local, there does not exist any comprehensive structure with members registered in a formal, or publicly available manner. We must rely upon efforts by well-established American polling agencies, in which questions are asked about (1) whether the individual maintains an affiliation to some part of the Tea Party Movement, or (2) whether the person simply supports the movement in an ideological sense. A large number of such surveys are available.

It is interesting to note that the demographics do not tend to paint the image that many people on the U.S. political left have hypothesized, namely that the Tea Party Movement is typically composed of white working class males with lower middle class incomes and no education beyond high school. In fact, while the Tea Party Movement activists and supporters do tend to be more white (about 80%, compared to 75% in the population as a whole, which means that about 1 in 5 supporters is not white) and male (55% male to 45% female, compared to 49% male in the general population), they also tend to be a bit wealthier and older than average. Their educational level, according to a Gallup poll, pretty much mirrors or slightly exceeds that of the nation as a whole, with only about 34% having no college education at all. A CNN poll indicated that nearly 75% of Tea Party Movement supporters attended at least some college. Geographically, while there is a higher proportion in the South and Midwest, than in the Western or Eastern states, significant support exists across the entire nation. In studies that have differentiated between active Tea Party Movement supporters and those who merely tend to agree with what they think of as the Tea Party Movement's perspective, the former are typically put at about 10% to 12% of the U.S. adult population, while the latter is estimated at an additional 22% to 24%. Thus, it seems likely that the Tea Party Movement is supported by 32% to 36% of adult Americans, about 1 in 3. If one were to describe the typical Tea Party supporter, the person would be white, male, older than 45, married, a bit wealthier and better educated than average and likely to live in the Midwest or South, but with significant representation across the nation. The key point is that at this level of support, this cannot be considered a fringe movement.

What Are the Key Ideological Elements Characteristic of the Tea Party Movement?

As described earlier, the fundamental undercurrent within Level One of the Tea Party Movement may best be described as libertarian and quite conservative. The tone expressed by the *Don't Tread On Me* flag captures this spirit. The common sentiments that are expressed over and over are keep the government out of my life, minimize government regulations, let the free market work, promote free enterprise (capitalism), reduce the size of government, cut taxes.

One of the first and still powerful catalysts for this entire movement was the Obama Administration's successful push for healthcare reform. Ironically, most Americans, and even many in the Tea Party Movement, hate the power and role of the health insurance industry and its often apparently arbitrary, but in fact cost/profit driven, decisions as to which care will be paid for and which not. And everyone resents the constantly increasing costs of health care. But the idea of the government mandating that everyone must have health insurance, or else pay a penalty to the government, drives the Tea Party Movement supporters absolutely crazy. They will not listen to arguments that without a mandate and a large pool of people, it is not possible to force the insurance industry to accept everyone without regard to prior conditions and without a surcharge for those with existing health problems. They will not listen to the fact that the plan includes provisions for the government to subsidize the poor and most of the middle class to help them afford the newly mandated health insurance premiums. They simply will not accept the idea of being forced to have coverage. While many resent the arbitrary power of the health insurance industry, they are furious that it will be the government that will make the new rules. Their resentment of government far outweighs their anger at industry.

Tea Party Movement supporters also were furious at the banks and the other financial institutions that caused the financial crisis and what has come to be called the Great Recession. But, at the same time, they deeply resented the fact that the government, first under Bush, and then under Obama, committed hundreds of billions of "their" dollars to "bail out" the banks and then to "stimulate" the economy. For Tea Party Movement supporters, the fact that the dire consequences of financial collapse were avoided and that the so-called bailout was conducted so that the government is on course to get every penny back is irrelevant. The banks were bailed out by government and their managers are again getting huge bonuses, while unemployment remains too high – so they judge the program a mistake. The fact that Obama's economic stimulus program largely worked, the collapsing economy was turned around, and 800,000 job losses per month was reversed to the point where jobs have been added every month for almost two years, is irrelevant. To Tea Party Movement supporters this all amounted to ineffective, socialistic government intrusion that has resulted in the largest government fiscal deficits (almost 10%) since World War II and a national debt that is approaching 90% of GDP. This feeds into a general conviction that government is simply too big and intrusive, spending is out of control, and taxes are too high (even though, in fact, taxes are far lower than during the Reagan period). Overall, surveys find that up to an amazing 99% of Tea Party Movement supporters express concern with the economy and with the government's economic policies.

At the same time, most Tea Party Movement supporters do not support cutting the Social Security or Medicare programs for the elderly. During the health care debate, one of the ironic cries was "keep the government's hands off my Medicare" – disregarding the reality that Medicare is a government program. This contradiction does not seem to cause discomfort. On the other hand, reflecting their economic status, Tea Party Movement supporters are quite willing to cut

Medicaid (a health insurance program for the poor), unemployment compensation, and a host of other programs that serve as the "social safety net."

Tea Party Movement supporters overwhelmingly do not believe that human behavior is causing climate change, or that climate change/global warming is a serious problem at all. Hence, they adamantly oppose government attempts to regulate emissions via a "Cap and Trade" system or any other program. Again, the presentation of scientific arguments is not persuasive. Just keep the government away from regulating industry or telling us what type of cars we should drive, are their cries.

There is mixed evidence pertaining to the ideological position of the Tea Party Movement with regard to social issues. Tea Party supporters tend to oppose illegal immigration and support strong anti-immigrant laws. They tend to be more likely to question Obama's religion (whether he is secretly a Muslim) and whether he was born in the U.S. than the general population. They are generally not supportive of so-called gay issues, especially gay marriage, but this is not a critical concern for them. There have been charges that elements of the movement display racist beliefs. This comes through most often when they argue against the need for programs to provide for the poor (hinting that the poor are mostly Black or Hispanic, which is not true) or when they talk about immigrants. While many of these social issues are core concerns for the broader conservative movement, these social issues are not the essential ideological elements that are important to the Tea Party Movement, and they are not the focus of their organizing efforts. The core beliefs of the Tea Party Movement are associated with reducing the size, spending, and reach of government. This movement is more libertarian in focus than traditionally conservative.

Is the Tea Party Movement an Effort to Spawn a New Political Party?

The answer is clearly no. In virtually every state and local area where this movement has emerged and self-identified with this title, it has viewed itself as an insurrectionist effort within the Republican Party. The rhetoric is consistently focused on the fact that the established Republican Party lost its way and "betrayed its principles" and the goals of the Tea Party Movement activists. They point to the unfunded expenditures of the Bush Administration and to the failure of Republicans in Congress to control government spending and reduce taxes. The perceived failure of the Congressional Republican caucus to stop the passage of Obama's programs was the final straw. Tea Party Movement activists believe that the Democratic Party is hopelessly too liberal, too progressive, even socialistic, and therefore not worth bothering with. They clearly do not have any desire, at least as of this writing, to undertake the very difficult task of organizing, funding, registering and getting recognition for a new party.

Instead, they intend to take over, dominate and re-direct the Republican Party. This type of effort is quite traditional in American politics. For example, the Anti-Vietnam War activists in the 1960s and early 1970s attempted to achieve the goal of dominating the Democratic Party and they, too, saw "their" party as having gone astray and needing to be re-directed. They did not bother trying to influence the Republican Party which they considered a hopeless task. So it has been in the case of the Tea Party Movement although it is the Democratic Party that is rejected.

Their entire effort in the 2010 Congressional elections was to run candidates within the Republican Party primary (preliminary) elections to determine who would run against the Democratic Party candidate in the general election. In some cases, they recruited and ran very conservative and/or libertarian candidates against established Republicans whom the Tea Party Movement considered too moderate, or just ineffective. In other cases, they decided to support a candidate, such as Rand Paul, who had already decided to run and who shared their ideology. In many cases, more established Republicans who "saw the writing on the wall," sought out their local Tea Party Movement activists and organizations, pledging their support for the Movement's principles in exchange for campaign support.

How Successful has the Tea Party Movement Been and What is Its Likely Future?
Since it began in late 2008, the impact of this

movement on American politics has been remarkable in Congressional and Senate electoral campaigns from coast to coast. This movement supported candidates in 138 Congressional races. Best estimates are that more than half of the 87 new members of the House of Representatives (a body of 435 people, all of whom have to run every two years) count themselves as Tea Party Movement supporters. Forty-nine Representatives joined the Tea Party caucus (led by Michele Bachmann) in the House. In the U.S. Senate, 13 Tea Party Movement candidates defeated establishment Republicans in primary elections and 7 went on to defeat Democrats and now serve in the Senate, where they will be for at least six years. Interestingly, some of the 6 that lost did so against Democrats considered easily beatable by established Republicans, most notably in Maryland and Nevada. In those cases, libertarian views were rejected and helped elect weak Democrats.

Local Tea Party Movement groups, supported and coordinated by Level Two and Three national organizations, have continued to agitate and demonstrate around their issues. Recently, they have supported efforts to remove collective bargaining rights from public sector employees on the state level, on the false premise that these employees "caused" government's fiscal problems. In fact, the motivation of the Level Two and Three organizations is to weaken the Democratic Party, which depends on these unions, prior to the 2012 elections.

What does the future hold for the Tea Party Movement? Where is it likely to go from here? It is important to note that the local and regional structures of the Tea Party Movement in 2010 were necessary to mirror the local Congressional District (House of Representatives) and State-wide U.S. Senate electoral battles. But in November 2012, there will be a national presidential election with Barack Obama as the Democratic Party's candidate. As the Republican Party moves to identify its candidate to oppose Obama, there will be electoral "primary" battles in most states. It is to be expected that the Tea Party Movement will participate in most of these and will attempt to identify its own preferred candidate(s) perhaps to the consternation of the more established Republican Party. If one of the Tea Party's favorites emerges as the Republican choice, the Tea Party Movement will quickly attempt to have both a national and state organizational presence to provide support. Given that American presidential elections are not decided by the national vote totals, but rather by state-by-state majorities (the Electoral College votes explained earlier) – the Tea Party Movement's regional structure that was so relevant in 2010 Senate and Congressional races, will again be important.

If, on the other hand, the Republican Party chooses a candidate that is not acceptable to most Tea Party Movement activists, then we will see a moment of truth. Do these activists support the Republican candidate as the best available route to defeating

Obama, whom they hate as a socialist – or do they attempt to organize a Third Party structure to oppose both established candidates? In 1968, this was exactly the plight of the Anti-Vietnam War movement. Their efforts to nominate Eugene McCarthy were thwarted at the Democratic Party's Chicago convention, and the party nominated Hubert Humphrey instead. Humphrey was a "good and committed liberal," but he had refused to break with Lyndon Johnson on the issue of the war. So, in state after state, including a major effort in California, attempts were made to run McCarthy as an independent candidate (there being no time to start and register a new official political party). While this effort was thwarted in most states, it drained a great deal of energy from the Humphrey campaign and greatly weakened his attraction. Some claim that the result was Richard Nixon's victory.

It remains to be seen what the Tea Party Movement activists will do in 2012 if they do not get a Republican presidential candidate of their choosing. It is far too early to predict, but it will be rather telling to watch.

This piece was also published in the Dutch journal Streven: A Journal of Political Economy.

To Frack or Not to Frack? (Issue #21)

By John Grula

The goods and the bads of fracking: and what needs to be done now

The natural gas and oil extraction process known as hydraulic fracturing, or "fracking," has been in the news as of late and become very controversial. If you think this article is going to make a knee-jerk environmentalist/left-wing critique of fracking, think again. It's a complex subject.

Fracking is a relatively new technique that uses large amounts of pressurized water, mixed with sand and chemical additives, to create fractures in shale rock located deep underground. The process frees trapped natural gas (primarily methane, which is comprised of one carbon atom chemically bound to four hydrogen atoms — CH_4 — and is gaseous in form) and some oil (longer polymers of carbon atoms which are liquid in form) and allows previously inaccessible natural gas and oil to be extracted from the Earth.

Natural gas is a versatile fossil fuel that is used for heating homes, cooking (think of your gas-powered stove and oven), electricity production, transportation and as an industrial feedstock for manufacturing plastics and other carbon-based materials.

Natural gas burns much more cleanly than other fossil fuels, such as oil and coal. Coal is by far the worst fossil fuel, and not only releases copious amounts of the greenhouse gas carbon dioxide (CO_2) when burned, but also other harmful chemicals, including mercury, arsenic and acid rain-causing compounds, (e.g. nitrates and sulfates).

When natural gas is burned it also releases CO2, but only half the amount released by burning coal per kilowatt-hour of electricity generated. To the extent we replace coal-burning power plants with natural gas-burning power plants (which is already happening), this will reduce CO2 production and help mitigate warming.

As a result of the increased use of fracking in recent years, the price of natural gas in the US has plummeted from a high of $12 per million BTUs in 2008 to the current low price of between $3 and $4. This has given a significant boost to the US economy. Substantial job gains have materialized from the expansion of the fracking process itself. In addition, manufacturing job growth has occurred when natural gas has been used, for example, as a feedstock for the synthesis of plastics and in its liquefied form is consumed domestically and also exported as a source of fuel. According to Daniel Yergin, author of the recent book, *The Quest: Energy, Security and the Remaking of the Modern World*, "This is fundamentally improving the competitive position of the United States in the world economy."

Having provided the upsides, here are some major downsides to fracking, especially in regard to the state of California. For starters, the process uses huge amounts of water, a problem that a water-starved region such as ours can ill afford. In addition, the harmful chemicals used in the fracking process can contaminate surface bodies of water as well as shallow aquifers that are crucial sources of drinking water. Plus, once the brine and chemical-laced water used for fracking is injected deep underground, it remains contaminated and is essentially lost for any other uses for perhaps hundreds of years or longer.

Another major problem with fracking and the natural gas it produces is leakage of the gas itself (again, mainly CH4) into the atmosphere and water supplies. CH4 is a very potent greenhouse gas and on a molecule-per-molecule basis traps much more heat than does CO2. But because the current atmospheric concentration of CO2 is about 400 parts per million, whereas CH4 comprises less than one part per million, CO2 is still the biggest problem. Nevertheless, CH4 leakage into the atmosphere is a major concern with respect to global warming and must be kept to an absolute minimum. CH4 is also highly explosive and any leakage into water supplies carries the risk of causing drinking water to become flammable and explosive.

Perhaps the clincher in the case against fracking in California is a recent report in the journal *Science* that increased fracking in the central and eastern US has led to a dramatic surge in the number of earthquakes in those regions. According to *Science*, three relatively large (magnitude 5.0 and larger) fracking-induced earthquakes struck near Prague, Okla., (normally a seismically inactive area) in November 2011. While 5.0 earthquakes are not large by California standards, it is also the case that small-to-moderately sized earthquakes can sometimes trigger much bigger earthquakes. The last thing California needs is a human activity such as fracking that can increase our risk of devastating temblors.

At the very least, Gov. Jerry Brown and the California Legislature need to declare an immediate moratorium on any further fracking in our state until all the risks are more clearly understood. That probably goes for the rest of the nation as well. This practice, which puts human and environmental health in jeopardy, while also continuing our dependence on fossil fuels, needs to be phased out as we phase in more renewable energy sources and increased energy efficiency.

This article was also published in the Pasadena Weekly on September 11, 2013

Fracking: While It's Dangerous, There's Money To Be Made, But Not By the People Asked To Live With It (Issue #22)

By John Grula

There is so much that is not understood about hydraulic fracturing (fracking) that, in view of the various dangers, a moratorium is needed – but then some people (corporations) are making quite good profits from the activity and so will fight to prevent that from happening.

Fracking is a technique that has been around for some 50 years, but it was rarely used until just the last five years or so. Therefore, contrary to oil company reassurances, we really don't have much experience with fracking and don't understand all the dangers it presents.

In recent years, the number of fracked wells and the amount of oil and gas extracted by fracking has exploded. While this has resulted in increased domestic oil and gas production, and substantially cheaper natural gas, the method is very controversial because of an array of hazards it presents to the health of people and the environment.

Fracking an oil or gas well involves injecting millions of gallons of water along with sand and various chemicals into rock formations at very high pressure. It results in breakage of the rock formations and keeps the rock open so oil and gas can be raised to the surface. One of the concerns about fracking that has arisen during California's current drought is the large amounts of water consumed and contaminated by fracking. Are there more important uses for this water other than extracting yet more oil and gas? Many Californians would answer "yes."

The list of hazards associated with fracking is rather lengthy: surface water contamination, soil contamination, wastewater disposal, air pollution, water supply threats, damage to natural habitats, and nuisances (noise, traffic, odors). Earthquakes are also cited as a potential threat that may result from fracking. However, earthquakes can be caused not so much by fracking itself, but by the common practice of re-injecting deep underground the highly polluted water created by fracking. Geologists say, on the basis of preliminary studies, that we need to take this threat seriously.

For instance there is a lot of fracking currently taking place in the Long Beach area. It is best then to remember that on March 10, 1933, the magnitude 6.4 Long Beach Earthquake took place. It killed 120 people and caused an estimated $50 million in property damage. This earthquake occurred along the Newport-Inglewood Fault, a fault which is still active and thought to be capable of causing another earthquake with a magnitude as large as 7.4. Such a quake would be catastrophic for the Los Angeles area.

How much do we know about whether or not there are re-injection wells used for Long Beach-area fracking waste water that are located near the Newport-Inglewood Fault? Not much. But this case illustrates the kind of danger we might be placing ourselves in because of fracking. If there is even a small chance that deep-earth re-injection of fracking waste water could trigger an earthquake along the Newport-Inglewood Fault (or the San Andreas Fault, as far as that goes), then we shouldn't be taking that chance. Let's place a moratorium (temporary delay) on fracking until we know much more about the science and the hazards.

Why are we in such a hurry to frack our state

when we clearly don't know enough about all of the potential dangers? Let's take a time-out and gain a much better understanding of fracking before we foolishly plunge ahead into possible disaster.

It should be noticed that there has been a 25-fold surge in oil shipments by rail in the last five years. These shipments have resulted in eight serious oil train accidents in the US and Canada in just the last year and in some cases the accidents caused spectacular fires and explosions. In the worst incident, last July in Canada, a train with 72 oil cars derailed and plowed into a town, exploded, killed 47 people and destroyed half of the town.

Californians won't take any comfort in knowing that more than 200,000 barrels of crude oil per month were imported into our state last summer by rail, a fourfold increase since 2012, according to a Los Angeles Times report in September.

Supporters of fracking primarily cite its alleged economic benefits. Of course, oil and gas companies stand to make considerable profits from the use of fracking, but these same companies also like to point to the potential for increased revenues to state and municipal governments and substantial job creation. But do oil industry claims about enhanced government revenues and job growth from an expansion of fracking really hold up to scrutiny? Let's examine the recent experience of the city of Carson.

Carson is a demographically diverse community of about 92,000 residents located in southwestern Los

Angeles County. Occidental Petroleum has proposed a massive oil project there and is seeking to drill more than 200 new wells in the northern part of the city, near California State University Dominguez Hills. On March 18, 2014, according to the LA Times, the Carson City Council unanimously passed a 45-day moratorium on all new oil drilling because of citizen outcry about the dangers presented by the Occidental project, especially the use of fracking.

However, on April 29, the Carson council failed to garner enough votes to extend the moratorium, in part because, unlike previous council meetings, supporters of the drilling project, many of them claiming to be union members with T-shirts and signs that read "Jobs for Carson," showed-up in large numbers.

How many jobs are we talking about? According to Carson City Councilman Albert Robles, there are only a little over 100 temporary jobs (such as construction), and less than two-dozen long-lasting jobs over the life of the project (estimated to be 30 to 40 years). And this is according to Occidental's own numbers.

Councilman Robles, who grew-up in Carson, is the first in his family to graduate from high school and he went on to obtain several university degrees (culminating with a *juris* doctorate from UC Berkeley). He's nobody's fool. He led the charge on the 45-day moratorium and voted to extend it. "When you've got 10,000 residents who live in their homes within a very short vicinity of that [Occidental] project and two-dozen jobs, it's a no-brainer to me," Robles is quoted saying in the Times. "But it's not about the jobs. It's about money [for Occidental]."

What about revenue to the city of Carson from the Occidental project? Again, according to Councilman Robles, city staff has estimated it would amount to roughly $1 million a year after the project ramps up to full capacity. This for a city that currently has an annual budget of about $70 million. This $1 million amounts to 1.4 percent of that annual budget — a pittance. So much for an economic boom for the city of Carson from Occidental's proposed oil drilling project.

I asked Councilman Robles if he agreed that Carson could be a microcosm for the entire state of California, which is constantly bombarded with oil industry hype about all the jobs and government revenue that will accrue from an expansion of fracking in our state. He answered "yes."

Big Oil has a powerful grip on the California Legislature, and that goes a long way toward explaining why multiple bills calling for a fracking moratorium died in 2013, despite the fact that Democrats held super-majorities in both the Assembly and Senate. Last year the Western States Petroleum Association ranked first in lobbying spending in the state: according to an LA Times report of official filings, the Association spent $4.7 million on lobbying. Chevron was close behind, spending nearly $4 million in 2013.

Versions of this piece were also published in the Pasadena Weekly on March 20 and May 21, 2014.

Why the Constitution Did Not Prevent the Military Industrial Complex (Issue #12)

By Ivan Light

The Constitution was intended to prevent a standing army. It failed miserably. Progressives must seek a return to the framers' intentions. (Ye Gods!)

It is now 52 years since President Eisenhower warned about the risk of an "unwarranted acquisition of power by a military industrial complex." In that 52 years, we have witnessed the maturation of the Frankenstein monster that Eisenhower feared. In addition to undermining the civilian economy and infrastructure of the United States, the damaging consequences of our warfare state include prodigal waste of human lives through the prosecution of useless and even counter-productive wars, all initiated on trumped-up grounds by the executive branch with the tacit or explicit concurrence of Congress. The military monster thus created is still strong and dangerous, and, unless defeated, it threatens finally to destroy both our liberty and our prosperity.

Reflecting on this disaster, the existence of which is not breaking news, I asked myself whether the framers of the U. S. Constitution were aware of the risk of creating a permanent garrison state, and, if so, how the framers proposed to prevent it?

In answer to the first question, it is clear that the

framers of the U. S. Constitution openly feared and hoped to prevent the existence of "standing armies in peacetime." Their repugnance to standing armies arose in part from their study of Roman history, and their awareness of the disastrous consequences of standing armies in that history. However, their repugnance to standing armies also arose from their understanding of Britain's Glorious Revolution of 1688, then only a century distant. To prevent the monarch from turning the armed forces against the British people, Parliament had lodged the entire legal right to raise and support armies in itself, stripping the monarch of this authority. Parliament jealously protected this exclusive authority over the military, considering it a bastion of British liberty. The framers of the Constitution intended that Congress should have the same exclusive and jealously safeguarded authority to raise, equip, and pay armies.

However, although the framers dreaded the creation of standing armies in peacetime, and hoped to prevent it, the U.S. Constitution has clearly failed to prevent the birth and metastatic development of the very warfare state the framers loathed. We have just what the framers hoped to prevent! How did this failure occur in the light of the framers' firm and conscious resolve to prevent it? Although an academic question, even a hazy answer may suggest ways for contemporary Americans to extricate ourselves from the clutches of the military industrial complex.

Writing in the *Federalist Papers* (numbers 24, 25,

26, and 34), Alexander Hamilton ably explained to contemporary skeptics just why the proposed Constitution, which is now our Constitution, could be relied upon to prevent the fearsome growth of standing armies in peacetime. Hamilton did not dispute the grave risk of standing armies in peacetime; he shared that concern; he just argued that the proposed Constitution would suffice to prevent that dreadful outcome. One of Hamilton's arguments was geographical in nature. Thanks to its geographical isolation, once the United States built a strong navy, the nation could rely on its navy to destroy invasion flotillas at sea. No foreign state could attack the United States by land. Therefore, since the United States would not need standing armies to prevent foreign invasions, there was no reason to fear the creation of standing armies in peacetime.

Hamilton, however, rejecting a standing army nonetheless wanted a standing navy. He reasoned that the United States would need a permanent and powerful navy to defend its international commercial interests. He observed that a standing navy would never turn against the people of the United States as might standing armies. A navy could not enslave the mainland. Hamilton was a strong supporter of the U. S. Navy for both reasons.

Hamilton's was a convincing argument at the time, but it plainly did not anticipate that the commercial and political interests of the United States would someday eventuate in a world-spanning empire whose defense would require the projection of military power overseas, not just naval protection against invaders. Neither Hamilton nor the other framers envisioned the United States as an imperial power with worldwide geopolitical and economic interests to protect and advance if need be by military force. Had the Vietnamese, the Iraqis, or the Afghans launched invasion flotillas directed against our coasts, the U.S. Navy would indeed have protected the United States at sea just as Hamilton expected. But Hamilton did not anticipate that the United States would use its navy (and air force) to land ground troops in Vietnam, Granada, Panama, Iraq, and Afghanistan in the pursuit of imperial ambitions. In effect, then, this geographical argument of Hamilton's proved defective in the long run because the republic became an empire, and the Constitution was built for a republic.

Hamilton raised another argument intended to set at ease disquiet and uncertainty about the ability of the proposed Constitution to prevent the creation of standing armies in peacetime. Hamilton's main argument depended heavily, as he himself acknowledged, upon the legislative history of Great Britain in the aftermath of the Glorious Revolution of 1688. Parliament had stripped the monarch of authority over the military, and Americans should take their cue from this enactment, Hamilton declared. As long as the exclusive authority to raise, pay, equip, and maintain armies rested in the legislature, Hamilton argued, the American people need not fear standing armies in peacetime. That is, they need not fear that the executive would turn the standing armies against the people in a tyrannical usurpation of power as, indeed, we now witness in both Syria and Egypt. Under the proposed Constitution, Hamilton observed, the people elected legislators who alone had the authority to raise and maintain standing armies. The Legislature was expected jealously to guard all its powers against encroachment by the President under the separation of powers theory. Therefore, the people could rely on legislators to prevent a power-crazed or megalomaniacal executive from unleashing military violence against them.

Curiously, Hamilton did admit one exception that threatened his argument. If there should arise "a combination between the executive and legislative in some scheme of usurpation," he acknowledged (*Federalist #25*), the consequences would be grave, and would include what he called trumped-up "provocations" intended to bait foreign nations into military responses. The foreign nation's reaction to our provocations would then justify standing armies. In other words, by creating a permanent fear of external military aggression, the federal government could wheedle from the American people the authority and the resources to support a permanent warfare establishment. Here was a nasty potential problem, Hamilton conceded, which, if it could not be solved, would imply, said he, that voters should reject the Constitution. Hamilton was so distressed by this possibility that, although a supporter of the Constitution, he would have preferred to see it rejected rather than accepted with a standing army.

Happily, Hamilton found and proposed a solution to the problem he posed. In his estimation, the likelihood of a combination of Congress and the President was exceedingly small. After all, he reasoned, such a legislative/executive combination would require time to mature, and it was exceedingly "improbable" (*Federalist #26*) that a legislature could persevere in such a self-weakening course over a lengthy time period. Even "one man, discerning enough to apprise his constituents of their danger" would suffice to terminate the odious collaboration of legislature and executive in standing armies in time of peace.

Hamilton was right in a limited sense but wrong in the big sense. We actually had the man Hamilton predicted. His name was Dwight David Eisenhower. But we also understand now, through bitter experience, that Eisenhower's Cassandra warning was not enough to protect the United States against the unwarranted growth of a vast military industrial complex over five long decades. In fact, a protracted collaboration of the legislature and executive in the maintenance of standing armies is exactly what followed Eisenhower's prescient warning. Congress surrendered its right to declare war, and ignored most recently the War Powers Act that limited the President's authority to commit troops abroad. This long train of events proves that the dreaded legislative collaboration in abrogation of its own powers and authority was actually much more probable than Hamilton realized in 1784. We now know that Hamilton's arguments were inadequate. The Constitution he proposed did not offer the people of the United States a secure protection against standing armies in peacetime.

The take-home message depends on one's mood. If one is in a pessimistic mood, the sad reality of our healthy military industrial complex and sick economy reminds one of classical Greek tragedy in which a tiny flaw in the youthful protagonist contains the seed of his or her final destruction decades later. Moreover, also as in Greek tragedy, destiny overrules human contrivances. The framers hoped to avoid standing armies in peacetime, and tried to prevent that outcome, but, despite their intentions, their republic could not evade this tragic outcome.

On the other hand, if in an optimistic mood, we can take courage from the direction in which the framers wanted to go. Our military industrial complex is legal all right, but it is hostile to the spirit of the Constitution and to the plain intentions of the framers. Americans still treasure the wisdom and insight of the founders. The founders are on our side in this political fight, and progressive people should invoke the founders' wisdom and intentions when debating this crucial issue of our times.

The Great Christian Religious Divide (Issue #6)

By Charles Bayer

The idea, maintained by constant media repetition, that the dominant religion in this country is by its very nature politically conservative is (and always has been) a piece of conservative fiction.

There are many ways to look at the historic divisions among religious bodies. In our generation this divide is showing up in pointed examples of the gulf between right-wing evangelicals and left-wing progressives. A couple of generations ago it was fundamentalists and modernists. Similar debates have gone on since the inception of Christianity.

While each of the characterizations had linguistic validity during a specific historic period, I suggest that there is another way to look at the issue.

On one hand, there have always been those who viewed Christianity—and I assume other religions— as belief in the absolute truth of doctrinal statements. The early writers of our historic creeds focused not only on the nature of doctrine, but also on the proper way doctrine was worded. In Nicea, Jesus was declared to be the same substance as God, not simply similar substance. At the same time, there were others who saw Jesus as the servant working in roadside monasteries and in a multitude of simple ecclesiastical communities, feeding the hungry, clothing the naked, giving sight to the blind and offering good news to the poor. While we might like to think that there were Christians simultaneously affirming both perspectives, a clear division most often existed. Heretics were not burned at the stake because they welcomed strangers, but because they varied in how they saw the sacraments.

Today's division takes a similar shape. On one hand, there are the literalists who insist that the nature of right religion as described in the Bible—or at least in specific passages they choose to quote—is the essence of faith. Believing is a matter of adherence to biblical or ecclesiastical truths. On the other hand there are those who affirm that the Bible, and all religious sensibility, defines actions to be taken in today's world.

The question arises as to the appropriateness of either persuasion being involved in electoral politics. Certainly there is no place for religious dogma or doctrine as the basis for political action. But on the other hand, can those who advocate action on behalf of the left out, the poor, the segregated and ostracized, justify their political support of these causes flowing from a religion-based ethic? Both evangelical conservatives and socially active liberals have a perfect right to be part of political discourse. Issues of justice, care of the nobodies, equal opportunity, support of the marginalized—or opposition to these matters—is not the sole perspective of any religion or religious group, but is shared with a great variety of persons of different religious faiths and those of no faith. Atheists, agnostics, humanists of all sorts affirm, or deny, these values. They are not sectarian, and therefore, as social perspectives they have a proper place in any political discussion.

Conservative religionists have every right to support capital punishment, war, anti-gay marriage laws, etc. as long as they do not insist that these positions should become law because of the priority of doctrine. Once these matters are proclaimed to be religious dogma and therefore must be obeyed by society, a dangerous border has been crossed. Is religion, therefore, a set of doctrinal absolutes, or is it a moral compass that points those of many persuasions to responsible ways to live and to relate to one's neighbors?

Perhaps the first amendment of the Constitution puts it most clearly. It details a prohibition against establishing a religion as part of the nation's legal identity, but guarantees the free right of religious practice. Calling for economic justice or affirming the rights of gays and lesbians is not asking that some religious doctrine becomes law. Insisting that schools teach creationism because it is Biblical, clearly violates the establishment clause. Working for a just society, or even the opposite, may flow from a sensibility, but it is speech protected by the free exercise clause.

Creating Fundamentalist Politics: Fundamentalist Religion (Issue #21)

By Charles Bayer

The conception of god for liberal Christians (and others) is not at all that of fundamentalist Christians (and others) – and therein are political differences.

Does religion matter in issues involving public policy? You bet it does! One's conception of god is a significant marker in how one views the issues confronting society.

If your notion of god is akin to that held by very conservative religion, you will likely espouse very conservative politics. Clearly those congressional districts and states that are dominated by the Tea Party have fundamentalist Christians as a significant source of right-wing support.

What makes for the relationship? For a long time I believed that conservative religion just got washed in with a political red tide. I am increasingly convinced, however, that religious commitments have been among the dominant influences in creating right-wing political systems, and that one's conception of god is a determining factor in the creation of political views.

Biblical fundamentalists in the antebellum South were adept at citing Bible passages which justified slavery – the justification for it was treated as coming straight from god's mouth. Following the Civil War and continuing through most of the 20th century, the Ku Klux Klan marched through America with the fiery "cross of Jesus going on before." The issue, however, is far deeper than the simple proclivity to use biblical snippets to prove a cultural point. The fundamental issue is one's understanding of god.

While today's Christian fundamentalists no longer espouse slavery or segregation, the question is rather the way their notion of god determines the way in which other issues that have clear political ramifications are understood by those with a fundamentalist conception of god. The fundamentalists' god tends to be a lawgiver, who sets down specific rules for life, blesses those who keep them and condemns those who do not. This god not only has a special set of demands and beliefs, but a special law-abiding people whom "he" blesses with both spiritual and physical abundance. God wants his followers to be prosperous, and will provide nature-defying miracles which he will lavish on the faithful. Financial abundance, therefore, becomes a mark of faithfulness. This prosperity gospel applies solely to Christians who have received Jesus as Lord and Savior. All non-believers are not only outside the ranks of the blessed, but are also doomed to eternal damnation.

The fundamentalists' god has also selected the United States as his nation of choice. That is why one commonly sees the cross and the flag together. God blesses our wars, and is a particular advocate of American capitalism—divinely sanctioned economics. The nation's sins are all sexual. It is not greed, violence or bigotry which activates his wrath, but abortion and homosexuality. Natural disasters can be directly attributed to a public violation of these sexual norms.

You don't have to take my word for that view: just tune in to any of the TV channels which feature popular religion.

The conception of god usually honored by liberal religion, a group ignored by most political pundits, is universal in his/her love, not confined to a particular people or a particular nation. Condemned are sins of greed, inequality, bigotry, violence and lovelessness. This idea of god welcomes those many others who would be despised by the fundamentalists. Barriers become bridges and the nobodies get the best seats at the divine banquet. Liberal religion's god, according to Catholic teaching, has a "preferential option for the poor." All the spiritual laws are summed up in love for god and others—all others.

Beyond American Christianity, religious fundamentalisms are bad news in any society. It is fundamentalist Muslims who have created the violence which has caused terror in the Near East and elsewhere. Jewish fundamentalism is one of the primary factors keeping Israel from being willing to take even modest steps in solving the Palestinian question.

Many young people have left organized religion because they tend to believe that religion itself is a captive of narrow unloving doctrines and institutions. And who can blame them? The prominence of those doctrines are what gives religion a bad name.

Describe the nature of the god you believe in, and you will probably have defined where you stand on most of the issues confronting the world. It is not that religion doesn't matter, but that it may matter far too much.

Sex as a Hobby, Perhaps in the Lobby (Issue #22)

By Merrill Ring

In the Hobby Lobby case there are larger cultural issues than those the majority's decision rested on.

This piece isn't another analysis of the supremely warped decision in what has come to be called The Hobby Lobby case. What I'm interested in is what Cultural Conservatives took the case to be about and what they think the decision accomplished.

The best expression of what those people thought was at issue and their praise of the decision come from a major right-wing blogger (Erik Erikson): in his eyes the decision established that "my religion trumps your 'right' to employer subsidized consequence free sex." There were also friend of the court briefs filed that argued that the Court should rule in favor of Hobby Lobby because it would constitute an impediment to the practice of what they call "consequence free sex".

Note: there may not be any such thing as 'consequence free' sex (or consequence free anything for that matter). What is hidden behind that phrase is sex without the worry of pregnancy. Pregnancy, of course, is what contraception is aimed at preventing –

to not be able to employ it makes the serious consequence of pregnancy a major problem.

I don't believe that the Justice Alito's majority opinion made any reference to what the *amicus curiae* briefs and the Cultural Conservatives took to be that issue. A concern with consequence free sex is thus not part of the legal issues but expresses a broader cultural theme: how do and should we regard (human) sexual desire and activity?

More narrowly, it is fairly clear that the conservative crowing about the decision is focused upon its presumed effect upon females, on their sexual activities. Even more narrowly the Cultural Conservatives are referring to unmarried women (and though possibly also adulterous married women) as now having, as a result of the decision, a hobble placed upon their sexual activities.

Of course, the hobble is not, given the claimed restrictions of the decision, as extensively applicable as the Cultural Conservative would like. But it is satisfying to them because it is at least a tiny victory in their objection to the historical drift in our attitudes to human sexuality.

For what this talk about consequence free sex reveals is that still lurking in the minds of the Cultural Conservatives are the ancient ideas that sex is disgusting, to be indulged in for procreation only, and that women are the tools of the devil in tempting men to have sex outside the bounds of marriage and familial procreation.

But we progressives, social democrats, left liberals, also have our views of the broader cultural theme – we are not just into more narrow economic, political, legal issues. (There is a long standing joke that American liberals want to win the economic argument but are pulling ahead only on the cultural issues – while the conservatives really want to win the cultural matters but end up on top only the economic issues.)

The ancient ideas still residing the minds of the Cultural Conservatives have long since been rejected. But in light of the re-appearance of topic of human sexuality in the good life, it is worthwhile for we progressives to remind ourselves of what our thinking on the topic is.

We have come to see that human beings are a kind of animal (let's settle for mammal now to avoid all kinds of problems), brought onto earth through evolution. We are not an agglomeration of a non-earthly psyche or soul hooked for some brief and disturbing period of time to a piece of matter.

Animals, including ourselves, are generally constituted to have a deep interest in reproduction, in creating future members of their species. We do this by sex, an activity which is central to our being animals and which consumes lots of our attention.

One way in which we human beings are different from most if not all other mammals (whether we are unique in this I have no idea, not being a biologist) is that females of the species are sexually receptive even when not capable of becoming pregnant. This opens the possibility of 'recreational sex'. (One of religious bent might even say that that is an activity God thus intended. By the way, all of this could be located in a religious context: many progressives are religious and subscribe to these views stated in secular terms here.)

Since sex is central to the kind of being we are and sex for both males and females can take place without aiming at procreation, it follows that sex without the aim of reproduction is natural for the kind of creature that we are.

Of course one of the further differences between ourselves and other animals is that we are capable of creating and do create, maintain and develop a very complex culture (a culture that is so complex that it can lead people to deny that we are animals.) As sex is a powerful force in animal lives, including our own, the culture we have created has to deal with it. Ways of dealing with it are highly various but typically include restraints on its expression. Historically, in our particular culture the chief way that it has been dealt with is by severe constraints on its expression.

These constraints, however, are fading, breaking down. That is what the conservatives want to stop. They think of the sexuality of human beings, especially females, as needing to be tightly controlled.

We progressives, however, thinking of people as biological creatures living within a culture, think that it is a good thing to have sex without the possibility of pregnancy. And whatever devices are invented to further that expression of our humanity are to be appreciated. And whatever cultural, legal, barriers there are to sexual expression need to be carefully monitored to see that they satisfy only appropriate ends and are not a denial of our nature.

The Hobby Lobby decision is a legal barrier to sexual expression and thus, rather than being welcomed, is something to be overturned, for that reason among others.

Taxation of Corporate Profits (Issue #3)
By Bob Gerecke

A detailed progressive argument that corporate taxes should be eliminated – with wealthy shareholders taxed instead.

On March 24, 2011, the *New York Times* reported that General Electric paid no taxes on its $14.2 billion in profits, more than a third of which it earned here in the U.S. In fact, rather than paying, the corporation received over $3 billion from the IRS.

Many other huge businesses successfully game the tax system to pay little or no taxes, although few do so as successfully as G.E. This gives the huge companies a competitive advantage over smaller businesses that have a smaller tax department to invent tax avoidance strategies or have fewer foreign operations to which they can shift their profits. The tax system encourages the big ones to invest outside our country and discourages them from bringing their foreign profits into the US. It provides an incentive for them to issue bonds instead of dividend-paying shares of stock, because they can deduct bond interest but not stock dividends; bonds are debt, and the existence of this debt increases the risk of bankruptcy during a recession. And by enabling them to avoid taxes on real profits, our system of corporate taxes decreases the government's ability to provide services and shifts the tax burden to the rest of us.

Meanwhile, wealthy investors – who, unlike us working people, hold their corporate shares outside of an IRA, 401K, 403B or other retirement plans – pay a lower tax rate on their profits than the rest of us do on our profits and even on our salaries, because of the myth that their profits have already been taxed at the corporate level. In addition, the wealthy can avoid tax on their profits during their lifetimes, because (unlike the middle class) they don't need to cash out all or most of their investments to fund their retirement. They are thus able to gift or bequeath their wealth to their heirs, largely tax-free. This ability to escape taxes on most of their investments further lowers their effective tax rate far below that of the middle class.

It is an outrage that income derived from wealth is taxed less than income derived from work done by the people who produce our goods and services. This also concentrates our country's wealth, which damages our economy in two ways: it weakens the ability of consumers to spend money and thereby to create jobs, and it provides an excess of investment capital, which generates speculation leading to bubbles and crashes. It also concentrates political influence and is already destroying our democratic republic, making it instead a plutocratic republic. Finally, it undermines morality and ethics by tempting many to seek great wealth for themselves at the expense of others.

Because of these consequences of the corporate tax system, I'm increasingly convinced that it's better to eliminate the corporate tax and instead to tax wealthy shareholders progressively and promptly. Here's a proposal to accomplish that.

First of all, the corporate tax should be abolished completely.

Secondly, capital gains and dividends should be taxed at the same rates as the earnings and retirement income of working people – employees, the self-employed and small business owners – or even at a higher rate, rather than at a lower rate as is done now.

Thirdly, in addition to taxing such investment income at an appropriate rate, our government should tax a shareholder's profits – for those shares not held in a retirement plan -- not only when the shares are sold but also, for shares still held at the end of the tax year, by valuing them on the last day, and by requiring that the gain or loss in value be reported for tax purposes. That gain or loss in value should be calculated from the end of the prior year or from the purchase date, whichever is later.

Shares held in retirement plans (such as a

pension, IRA, 401k or 403b) should be exempted from this end-of-year taxation. After all, these plans are supposed to be tax-deferred, i.e., taxed only upon withdrawal. In this way, the middle class will not have to report income until withdrawals are made and will be taxed only on the value of the withdrawal, just as is done now. They will not have to sell shares and make a withdrawal from their plan – or take money out of their budget -- in order to pay a tax bill, and the value of their shares will not be reduced by a tax debt incurred before they sell them to make a withdrawal. For them, nothing will change.

By taxing the appreciation of shares held outside of retirement plans, this system will inhibit the accumulation of great wealth tax-free by those – primarily persons with inherited wealth or very high incomes -- who have invested far more than the maximum allowed in retirement plans. Under the present system, they can completely avoid taxes on their profits. They can let all or most of their investments grow indefinitely, because they have so much income that they don't need to cash out investments in order to cover their living expenses. They can then pass millions of dollars worth of investments directly to their heirs free of estate tax and indirectly to their heirs through various trusts.

To ensure that the upper middle class saver is not forced to sell shares to pay the tax, the allowable annual contributions to an IRA can be increased retroactively, allowing transfer of currently-held shares into the plan. The profits when these shares are kept or sold will then be tax-deferred until withdrawals are made in retirement, as if they had been originally purchased in a retirement plan. This will differentiate between the middle class and the truly wealthy.

Accumulation of wealth by the middle class will not be penalized or discouraged, but concentration of wealth in the hands of the economic elite will be more difficult, and taxation will be fairer. Both of these are ethically and socially desirable and necessary to preserve our democracy.

A corporation's incentive to boost earnings and cash flow will remain. The incentive to game the tax system will be obsolete. Loopholes at the corporate level will cease to exist. It won't matter whether the profits are from one type of business activity or another, and whether they are made in the US or overseas. In fact, it won't even matter whether the corporation is domiciled in the US or in another country; the US shareholder will be taxed in any case on the appreciation in value of his shares – whether he sells them or not -- and on any dividends received, as long as the shares are held outside of a retirement plan.

Shares held in IRAs, 401Ks and other tax-deferred retirement plans will still defer the tax; this is what these accounts are supposed to do, whereas under the present system their shares are taxed annually at the corporate level, which is not deferred, if the corporation actually pays taxes.

This should be a progressive tax, i.e., high-income

shareholders should pay a higher ordinary income tax rate on their share of the company's profits than lower-income shareholders will. This will be unlike the present corporate tax system, in which the small investor's shares are taxed at the same corporate rate as those held by the wealthy investor. Even worse, under existing tax law, capital gains and dividends from shares held by middle-class working people -- usually in a IRA or other retirement plan -- are eventually taxed at the higher ordinary income rate than those held by the upper class -- usually outside of such a plan -- which are taxed at the lower capital gains rate. Multi-billionaire investor Warren Buffett should no longer pay a lower tax rate than his middle-class secretary.

It will prevent the wealthy from escaping taxes on their profits by holding their shares until death and then passing them to their heirs tax-free. Middle-class working people can't do that, because they need to cash in their shares in order to produce income during retirement. The wealthy will no longer be able to increase their fortunes by leaps and bounds by not paying taxes on their gains. This will reduce or even reverse the growing inequality in income and wealth.

Corporations will no longer have a corporate tax incentive to issue bonds instead of dividend-paying shares, because they will no longer be in the position of being allowed a tax deduction on bond interest but not on dividends. This will, in some cases, reduce corporate borrowing and therefore the riskiness and volatility of stock shares. With less debt, fewer corporations will fail during recessions.

Corporations will no longer have to spend money on tax specialists or on lobbying for tax benefits, nor will they distort operations in order to avoid taxes. They will be more efficient. In addition, by not having to pay taxes, those companies which are now paying them will be more profitable and will have more cash flow to re-invest in the business or to pay dividends. Small & medium-sized and merely large businesses will no longer have the competitive disadvantage of being unable to game the tax laws the way that huge businesses like G.E. do. Those that now dutifully pay U.S. taxes will no longer be at a disadvantage to foreign corporations domiciled in countries which have little or no corporate tax. The vast majority of U.S. businesses will benefit.

So will the vast majority of Americans who invest in them, who work for them or who are dependents of those who do, because businesses which are more efficient and more successful will generate more profits and hire more employees, and because businesses which are not tax-penalized for investing and profiting in the U.S. will be more likely to do so. Companies will no longer have a tax incentive to keep their foreign profits out of our country and invest them elsewhere.

Congress can set the progressive personal tax rates on corporate share sales, appreciation and dividends, and the retroactive increase in allowable IRA contributions, to ensure that the resulting revenue increases, decreases or is neutral to the amount of revenue which the government now collects from the combination of corporate and investor income taxes. Because of the growing national debt, higher revenue is a desirable alternative, especially if it occurs at the expense of the wealthiest investors: they have been cornering the benefits of our economic and political system, they therefore can well afford to pay accordingly, and they have an obligation in fairness to do so. Even many of the wealthy agree with this and have formed a group to lobby patriotically for higher taxes on themselves.

The "Jobless Recovery" in the U.S.: What Happened to the Jobs and to Wages & Why? And What Can be Done? (Issue #22)

By Andy Winnick

For a comprehensive account of where the U.S. economy now stands and why and what should be done, read this article.

Some Background

The term "jobless recovery" has entered the vocabulary of those concerned about the current state of the U.S. economy as it applies to the employment situation in the aftermath of the recent recession (which officially extended 19 months from December 2007 to June 2009). The term "jobless recovery" reflects a concern that while the overall U.S. economy, as measured by the Gross Domestic Product (GDP: roughly the total dollar value of all goods and services produced within the United States in a year) has been growing since the third quarter of 2009, the number of jobs created and the total number of those employed through the end of 2013 has not increased at anything remotely close to the same rate. In fact, jobs continued to be lost for 10 months after the official end of the recession, until March 2010 when the U.S. saw the first monthly net increase in jobs since January 2008. The U.S. economy suffered a net loss of jobs for 25 consecutive months from February 2008 through February 2010. There was a net loss of jobs again from June through September 2010, 16 months after the official end of the recession.

In total, from February 2008 through February 2010, the U.S. lost a total of more than 8.7 million jobs. However, from then through the end of 2013, the U.S. added only 7.6 million, for a net loss of 1.1 million jobs. But that is the tip of the iceberg, because the U.S. needs about 150,000 new jobs per month simply to keep up with the normal increases to the working age population. So starting from when the job losses began in 2008 through the end of 2013, the U.S. needed 10.7 million new jobs to accommodate population growth, in addition to needing to make up for the 8.7 million lost jobs. (This is consistent with the official figures for the increase in the adult civilian population from 234.7 million in January 2009 to 244.4 million in December 2012.) So the net shortfall in job creation as of the beginning of 2014 is in the area of 12 million jobs.

The disparity between the jobs picture and the growth in the overall economy is reflected in the fact that by 2011, GDP (whether measured in current or in inflation-adjusted dollars) was already far higher than before the recession, and corporate profits reached historic highs by the end of 2011 and have continued to increase. On the other hand, the unemployment rate at the end 2013 was nowhere close to its pre-recession level of 4.4% in May 2007. In fact, it reached a peak of 10.1% in October 2009, five months after the official end of the recession. That is, the unemployment rate continued to increase long after the official end of the recession in June 2009. By June 2011, two years after the end of the recession, the unemployment rate still stood at 9.1%, only 1% point below its peak of 10.1%. By December 2013, four and a half years after the recession, it had only fallen to 6.7% -- which was still 52% higher than the rate in May 2007. (It should be noted that the unemployment rate comes from a survey of households; whereas the number of jobs/employment figures come from a survey of employers. So there is sometimes some inconsistency between the two figures in the short run, but over the longer run they tend to show quite consistent results.)

Not only has the unemployment rate remained high, but the nature of those unemployed has set historical records. If someone is laid off, but within a few months finds a new job, that is one thing. But if someone suffers a job loss, but then, despite vigorous efforts, cannot find another for more than six months, a year, two years, that is a very different situation. The percentage of those experiencing what is referred to as long-term unemployment set new records during and in the years after this Great Recession. Not since the 1930s has the U.S. seen such a high proportion of the unemployed unable to find a job despite many months, even years of looking. The country reached a point where there were seven people "officially" (see the discussion in the next section) unemployed for every job vacancy. That ratio remained at 3 to 1 at the end of 2013. In fact, the real ratio was much worse as we shall see. As a result, unemployment benefits had to be extended from the usual twenty-six week period to ninety-nine weeks, a new record. But then, at the end of 2013 these extended unemployment benefits were abruptly cut off, immediately devastating the families of 1.3 million long-term unemployed, with another 3 to 5 million who would have become eligible in the next few months, who now will not. And it is important to note that the dollar value of unemployment benefits in the U.S. as a percentage of the previously earned wages runs at about half of what is paid in the major EU nations.

It is no surprise that the long-term nature of unemployment has been devastating for millions of U.S. families. Millions had to use all of their normal savings and even their retirement monies. They could not qualify for loans of any sort and millions lost their homes. The terrible impacts of this long-term unemployment on physical and mental health, marriages, and family violence have been well documented and will have life-long consequences. Many young people have seen their lives stymied. Among those graduating from university, most of whom found some work, only 40% could find jobs even remotely related to what they had studied. Their professional careers are likely to be permanently damaged even as the economy improves, as they have to compete with more recent college graduates. Studies have shown that for people of all ages, the longer they remain unemployed the less likely they are to find work. Employers are using long-term unemployment as a screening criterion. Even for college graduates who worked, but did so outside the usual definitions of their career paths, the probability of their getting back on that path goes down the longer their out-of-field employment lasts.

The Impact of How the Term "Labor Force" is Defined

All of these concerns are magnified when one realizes that the unemployment rate is measured as a percentage of the "labor force", not as a percentage of the population over age 16 or even age 16-64. The labor force is defined as those who are working at least half-time plus those who are "officially" unemployed. To be "officially" unemployed, one must be working less than half-time or not at all, but be able, willing and actively seeking work. The Labor Force Participation Rate (the percentage of the adult population that is in the labor force) has fallen steadily since early during the recession; in fact, it has continued to fall for the four and a half years since the end of the recession – reaching 62.8% in December 2013, its lowest level since 1978. It is this shrinking labor force participation that is a major cause of why the unemployment rate has declined. That is, the unemployment rate has fallen in part due to the net creation of new jobs, but it also declined in large measure due to people dropping out, or being forced out, of the "labor force."

A good example of how these trends interact is what happened in December 2013. The number of new jobs created that month was 74,000, only half of what was needed to accommodate the usual flow of new entrants to the labor force and nowhere close to the 185,000 to 200,000 that had been occurring earlier that year. Nevertheless, the official unemployment rate dropped from 7.0% to 6.7%, the lowest rate since the early months of the recession in 2008. So some people pointed to that as a sign the economic recovery was doing well. But the only reason the unemployment rate fell at all was that 347,000 dropped out of the labor force entirely, at least as it is officially defined. So, the overall picture was decidedly negative that month, despite the fall in the unemployment rate. The picture was made even worse when it was revealed that the largest group exiting the labor force were age 45-54, the usual prime age for workers, causing the labor force participation rate for this age group to drop to its lowest level since 1988, almost a quarter of a century earlier.

When one takes into account some of those who have left the official labor force, but who still want work (often referred to as "discouraged workers", "marginally attached workers" and those working part-time who want full-time employment), the December 2013 unemployment rate more than doubles from 6.7% to about 14%. There is evidence that beyond the people enumerated above, there are many others who retired early, not by choice, but simply because they finally gave up ever finding a job. This consideration further raises the rate of real unemployment at the end of 2013 to well above 20%. Finally, there is also evidence that some workers in the 55-64 age group who had been looking for work unsuccessfully get cooperative doctors to certify them as disabled. With this certification, they qualify for Social Security Disability payments enabling them to survive on those payments until they reach retirement age. So clearly, while the U.S. economy as a whole has grown considerably since the recession, reaching historic new highs in GDP, and while there have been some improvements with regard to employment, the job situation remains far worse than before the recession.

Nevertheless, the term "jobless" is somewhat misleading. Rather, it is the case that too few jobs have been created for those needing and wanting them. When one combines an examination of even the official unemployment problem (which depends on the definition of the "labor force") with that of the shrinking proportion of the working age population that is in the labor force, it is clear that there continues to be a severe shortage of jobs in the U.S. four and a half years after the end of the recession. (However, it must be noted that the situation in the U.S. is nowhere near as severe as in many European nations.)

It's Not Just the Number of Jobs, but the Wages and Benefits

Aside from the issue of the number of jobs that have been created, there is a major problem associated with the nature of those jobs. Far too often, the new jobs carried much lower wages, as much as 50% lower, than those that were lost, and too often these new jobs were only for part-time work. In fact, real (adjusted for inflation) hourly and weekly wages in the U.S. for all "non-agricultural and non-supervisory" workers (which account for more than 80% of all workers in the U.S.) were less in 2013 than they were in the early 1970s – 40 long years ago.

Moreover, many of the jobs that were lost, especially those in manufacturing, had come not only with good wages, but also with good pension plans. But most of the new jobs had either no pension plan at all, or only had defined contribution plans (to so-called 401k programs in which small amounts of money are put into the stock market by employers on behalf of employees) rather than defined benefit plans where a specific amount or percent of old-age income is guaranteed. In addition, the lost jobs, especially those in manufacturing, typically carried good health insurance benefits, whereas many of the newly created jobs carried either no health insurance at all, or provided only far more limited plans. All of these factors have reduced the income of many of those lucky enough to have found new jobs, and left them with much less security for when they get ill or retire. (The new health insurance programs going into effect in 2014 as part of the Obamacare – Affordable Health Care Act – program will begin to address some of these issues.)

As a result of these trends, the "real" (adjusted for changes in prices) median (middle) level of household income in the U.S. (which is the preferred broader measure than family income, since it includes all those living together in a household even if they are not all related by marriage or birth) dropped by more than 10% from January 2008, at the beginning of the recession, to January 2011 – a year and a half after the official end of the recession. Since then, it has increased only very modestly through 2013, when it still remained about 9% below the January 2008 level and 8% below the level way back in January 2000.

Less someone thinks that this is totally a function of the education of the head of the household, it is important to understand that for households headed by someone with only a high school education, median income had dropped from the official end of the recession through June 2013 by 9.3%, for those with a 2-year college certificate it dropped by 8.6%, and for those with a 4-year college degree by 6.5%. So more education slowed the rate of decline, but it did not stop it.

As usual in the U.S., there is also an important ethnic element to what has happened to real household income from the official end of the recession to June 2013 – 4 years later. White, non-Hispanic households saw a 3.6% drop in median income, Hispanic households dropped 4.5%, and Black, non-Hispanic households dropped a staggering 10.9%.

Inequality and Distributional Effects

A related problem is that during this recovery period, the already very wide disparities in income between the richest 1% and everyone else (about which I have written extensively in an earlier article about the Occupy Movement), widened considerably as a result of the fact that 95% of the increased income generated during the recovery period went to the richest 1% of U.S. households. Closely related to this is the fact that while corporate profits, especially in the financial sector, increased to record highs, the percentage of total income going to wages and salaries fell to historic lows. It should be noted that most of the income of the richest 1% comes from the profits of business, stock dividends, capital gains, and so-called "carried interest" – not from wages and salaries, despite the fact that CEOs of large firms earn tens and even hundreds of millions of dollars per year in salary.

Closely related to the growing inequality is the stagnation in economic and social mobility. The U.S. is in love with the myth of "rags to riches," with the idea that it is "the land of opportunity," where as a result of hard work, self-improvement, and perseverance anyone can go from poverty to wealthy. But the sad fact is that this myth is no longer valid. The extent of socio-economic mobility in the U.S. has stagnated for decades and is the lowest of any nation for which we have data. In fact, what is now being studied in the U.S. is the pattern of "rags to riches to rags in three generations" where many upper middle class families are doing far better than the grandparents, but where the children are slipping back below the economic level of their parents.

Turning to the Issue of Why

We have identified the problem: namely, there are currently too few jobs paying far too little in wages and carrying very weak benefits to provide an adequate level of economic support to 90% of American households. Associated with that is the widely and well documented fact that the inequality gap in both income and wealth in the U.S. has been widening for 40 years (since the early 1970s) and is now at a level that had not been seen in the U.S. since the Roaring 1920s. Some even compare the present period to the excesses of the Gilded Age of the 1870s and 1880s.

That leaves us with the really important questions:

- Why has the U.S. economy not been generating a sufficient number of jobs to bring the unemployment level back down to a level reasonably considered as full-employment, such as 4 to 5%?
- Why has the proportion of long-term unemployment remained at historically high levels?
- Why has the proportion of the adult population in the labor force fallen to historically low levels?
- Why have real hourly wages stagnated and even fallen since the early 1970s?
- Why has median household income not even begun to keep pace with increases in GDP and has even fallen for sustained periods during which the economy grew?
- Why has the extent of inequality widened rather consistently since the early 1970s?
- Why has socio-economic mobility completely stagnated at a comparatively low rate?
- And how are all these trends connected?

These are the issues to which we now turn.

Then there are the remaining two questions which become of paramount importance:

- Are there steps that could be taken to correct these problems, and if so, what are they?
- How likely, or even possible, is it that these corrective steps will indeed be taken?

Trying to Answer Some of these "Whys?"

The fundamental issues are how can the U.S.

economy show considerable growth in economic production and in corporate profits, while at the same time the number of jobs increases so slowly that the real unemployment rate remains high, the proportion of the working age population that is even in the labor force (employed or unemployed) shrinks, and wages and household incomes stagnate or fall? To understand this current situation, it is necessary to briefly look back at how we arrived at this point.

The Role of the Growing Gap between Wages and Productivity -- The Collapse of Private Sector Unions

One core cause is that advances in technology and communications have enabled the productivity of labor to steadily increase. From 1945-1973, the increases in productivity resulted in the increases in output and revenue being shared between the owners of capital and their workers – allowing for higher wages, shorter work-weeks, and proportionate increases in profits. But what has been happening instead since the mid-1970s is that while productivity continued to increase, wages and the work-week stagnated, while profits increased and production expanded. But that statement begs the question of why this has happened. And here the analysis gets more complicated.

Some of the causes of this new pattern reflect internal changes within the U.S., others are the result of new and accelerating systems of economic globalization. On the domestic front, what has been happening for the last 40 years in the U.S. is a steady decrease in the proportion of the private sector work force that is unionized. It was always the unionized workers who, when labor productivity increased, would use that fact to push for higher wages, better benefits and fewer hours of work. Their argument was that this increase in productivity would compensate for the increase in labor costs and still allow for higher profits. Until the mid-1970s this strategy was successful and wages and productivity went up in close parallel. But the proportion of the private sector labor force (as opposed to the public or government sector) that is unionized has been steadily dropping in the U.S. For the private sector, the rate of unionization dropped from 36% in the 1950s to just 6.6% by the end of 2012. This is the lowest rate in 76 years, since 1936 in the depth of the Great Depression. The overall rate of unionization dropped to 11.3%, but this higher figure is due entirely to the fact that the public sector workers' unionization rate has held at 35.9%. On a state basis, New York had the highest overall rate, 23.2%, while North Carolina had the lowest, 2.9%.

This compares to the experience in other industrialized democracies where Finland, Denmark and Sweden have the highest rates of unionization (in 2010-11: 69%, 69% & 68%), Belgium: 50%, Germany: 18% (which also has a system of Worker Councils). The only major nation with a lower rate than the U.S. is France, 7.8% in 2010.

Private sector workers in the U.S. were thus left without the means to continue to secure reasonable increases in wages and compensation (wages plus benefits). Political conservatives always complain that liberals talk about a class war that never happened. The liberals say that there has indeed been a class war, and workers lost it. Since 2000, a new war has broken out in which Republicans at the state and national level have now begun a major campaign to destroy the public sector unions, in an attempt to imitate what they have already achieved in the private sector.

The business community has taken much of the extra profits they have secured by holding wages down and spent that money on new technologies that would enable them to greatly reduce the labor force, so that they can produce more goods with fewer workers earning lower wages. This has allowed them to create a more competitive position, especially relative to other developed nations. Indeed, the U.S. has become such a low-wage nation that Germany builds factories in the U.S. to reduce costs and desperate, non-unionized U.S. workers clamor for the low wage jobs. Firms have also used these profits to shift major elements of their productive assets abroad in order to set up factories in developing nations where foreign workers earn a fraction of even the stagnant wages in the U.S. This enabled them to further reduce the U.S. work force. This process has greatly accelerated in the last 20 years, since the mid-1990s.

If Wages Have Been Stagnant Since the mid-1970s, How

Could Consumption Remain at 70% of an Increasing GDP or Who Can Buy the Increased Production if Wages are Stagnant?

The answer to this conundrum has three stages. First, as wages were held constant, families could only increase their standard of living by a worker taking on a second job, or by moving from one paid worker per household to two and even more. Starting in the 1950s, and then accelerating in the mid-1970s, the labor force participation rate for women increased dramatically from 34%, reaching a peak of 60% in 1999. During this same period the labor force participation rate of males dropped steadily from 86% to 73%. In fact the increase in the overall participation rate from 1975-1999 was entirely due to the increased participation of women. When that began to hold steady or even decrease a bit (in part as some of the older women began to retire), the overall rate began to drop quickly, reaching 62.8% at the end of 2013.

But once the women had entered the labor force, and wages for both men and women stagnated, something new was needed to sustain any increase in consumption. The financial sector stepped in and began developing new tools to increase consumer debt, especially credit cards. Soon consumer debt began to increase dramatically, enabling families to sustain and increase their consumption, but at the cost of taking on massive debts at often very high interest rates. As a result the net wealth of most American families fell and for many of them, especially in the minority communities, became negative. On the other hand, the banks enjoyed the resulting new sources of revenue, the manufacturing and service industries enjoyed higher levels of demand and revenue, households enjoyed a higher apparent standard of living, but only by assuming the risks and costs of taking on these massive levels of consumer debt.

But by the late 1990s and early 2000s, this mountain of consumer debt reached unsustainable levels, so something new was again needed to shore up consumer demand, and the financial system came up with a new, dangerous, but temporarily effective device. They invented a wide variety of new types of home mortgages, many of them considered "sub-prime," meaning they violated the usual norms of safe lending. Mortgage loans were made at artificially and temporarily low interest rates to consumers many of whom represented what would normally be considered bad risks. As a result, there was an unsustainable increase in the demand for housing which caused a housing price bubble from 2000 to 2007. Home-owners were encouraged to turn the artificially increased value of their homes into cash to support consumer demand via a whole series of financial instruments such as home equity loans. This provided a way to sustain and increase consumption based upon nothing more than artificially created higher prices for homes. But in March 2007, the bubble burst (as many, including this writer, predicted it must and would), and the Great Recession began a few months later. Now, without some new device in place, consumer demand and GDP fell, and unemployment dramatically increased. No such new device has yet to come on the scene domestically, and so the economy limps along, growing at historically low rates with high levels of employment.

Globalization

In the last 20 years or so, economic globalization has been spurred on by dramatically lower international communications costs (via communication satellites, cell phones and the internet), containerization and larger, faster ships which brought shipping time and costs down, internationally linked financial institutions which expedited the global movement of money, and computerization/robotization of production which allowed the rapid spread of productive technology. This has led to the U.S. labor market becoming divided into three new categories.

1. The financiers, facilitators and organizers of international commerce who have experienced unprecedented increases in their personal income and wealth and in the profits of their corporations, and who have sustained high incomes in comparison to those providing luxury services to them.

2. Those in the tradeable goods manufacturing and service industries who must compete directly with those in other nations who can and do produce those same goods and services at far

lower costs, enabling them to undercut their American counterparts. This results in continuous major trade deficits, and in lost jobs and lower wages in these industries in the U.S. For example, the U.S. lost almost 6 million manufacturing jobs between 2000 and 2009, but has gained back only 568,000 since January 2010. Moreover, since the end of the recession in 2009, manufacturing wages have dropped 10%.

3. Those in the non-tradeable goods and service industries, who are not in direct international competition. However, as workers from the tradeable sector are laid off, they often seek employment in the non-tradeable sector, forcing wages there lower and squeezing out many of these workers.

The result is that 80-90% of U.S. workers have experienced stagnant wages, and now, in the aftermath of the Great Recession, families face high levels of unemployment and low levels of labor force participation. At the same time, those in the first group have enjoyed all the benefits of the growth that has occurred in the form of astronomically higher salaries, income from other sources and vast increases in wealth.

The Growing Schism Between the Rich and the Rest
This schism between the very rich and the rest

has been perpetuated and reinforced. A new Gilded Age has emerged in the U.S., rivaling, indeed exceeding, that of the 1880 &1890s and of the Roaring 1920s. The richest 1% saw its share of the nation's income drop from 23% just before the Great Depression to "only" 12% in the 1970s, then turn around to reach almost 24% in 2013. Its share of national wealth has increased to the unprecedented level of more than 80% of all non-residential wealth. Another way to look at this schism is to note that a new study (Fazzari and Cynamon) showed that in 2012 the richest 5% accounted for a new high of 38% of all consumption expenditures in the U.S., which was about equal to what the bottom 80% accounted for at 39%. U.S. businesses have acknowledged this pattern by expanding the markets for luxury goods and services, while cutting back on those for the shrinking middle class and maintaining those for families under economic duress. To see one aspect of this pattern on the economy, consider that if a rich family buys a car that costs four times as much as a car bought by a middle-class family, production of that expensive car does not generate four times more jobs. Indeed, that luxury car is likely to be imported and generate no manufacturing jobs in the U.S. at all. A lower-class family can only afford a used car, the purchase of which also generates no additional manufacturing jobs. It is clear that this growing concentration of income, wealth and consumption has a seriously dampening effect on wages and employment.

But this schism is far more than economic. A

major study (Wilson) that focused on European Americans ("Whites") to abstract from comparisons with the African, Hispanic, and Asian-American communities, found that rich Whites experience totally different lives for themselves and their children than the rest of even White society. Their children go to private pre-schools, elementary and secondary schools that cost tens of thousands of dollars a year, and then go on to elite private universities that cost in excess of $60,000 a year. They live in vastly different and safer communities, belong to expensive clubs, eat different foods at home and in restaurants, have many servants and house workers, vacation in far different places, and travel extensively internationally. But perhaps most importantly, the rich, and especially the super-rich, are able (especially given recent Supreme Court decisions) to use their wealth to control much of the political process from the selection of candidates, to elections, to lobbying for laws, to influencing the implementation of laws via control of the regulatory process. This is often true at the local, state and national level. For example, this political control helped to create the legal climate that was instrumental in supporting corporate efforts to destroy trade unions in the private sector, and is now supporting the attack on public sector unions.

Meanwhile, the poor and near poor, most of whom work full time at very low wages, live desperate lives in often dangerous communities kept from starvation and homelessness only by social welfare programs that are constantly under attack by conservative forces. The official poor account for about

15% of the population and the near poor for an additional 15% to 20%.

But the biggest effect since the mid-1970s has been the plight of the shrinking and ever more desperate middle class. Poverty and near poverty is now growing far faster in the suburbs than in the inner cities. Official government studies (Census Bureau) reveal that for 3 to 6 or more months in any five-year period fully 80% of U.S. families experience either (a) unemployment or (b) such low wages that they have to turn to social welfare programs to obtain food and/or pay their rent, or (c) are devastated by medical expenses that drive them into bankruptcy or poverty. To the best of my knowledge, no other industrialized democracy subjects such a large proportion of their population to such economic distress. (As noted earlier, Obama's new health insurance programs will reduce the danger of medically induced poverty and bankruptcy.)

Many of them turn to higher education in an attempt to escape this fate. But despite financial aid programs for the poorest, relatively few of them graduate from college. The middle class kids who do not qualify for financial aid must take on massive student loans to get a college education – to the extent that the total student loan burden in the U.S. now exceeds the total of all credit card debt. In fact, student debt increased by 500% from 1999 through 2013, while starting salaries for new graduates dropped by 10%. Repaying these loans severely limits their consumption and home buying for 20 years or more following graduation. All of these factors, as we have seen, have held back socio-economic mobility in the U.S. to the extent that it has become one of the world's most rigidly stratified industrialized democracies, defying the old myth of American as "the land of opportunity" for those already here – while still being a destination of choice for immigrants from even lower-wage nations.

Does a Solution to These Problems Exist?

The answer is a resounding Yes! And many economists, sociologists, political scientists, and physical scientists are agreed as to what is needed. It is a fairly straight-forward seven step program.

1. Fix the labor market: Set the minimum wage at 50% of the median wage, and adjust it to the inflation rate as we do for Social Security. Change the legal structures to encourage unionization, or at a minimum the creation of German-style worker councils to consult regularly with management on all major decisions. Restore the relationship between changes in productivity and changes in wages by reestablishing the expectation that they should move about in parallel, requiring firms to justify themselves when that does not happen.

2. Begin a 20-year program to restore, rebuild and modernize the infrastructure of the U.S.: Civil engineers agree that more than two-thirds of the bridges and overpasses are structurally deficient and urgently need to be repaired or replaced. Highways are in sad shape.

There is not one mile of high speed rail for passengers or freight. The old and deteriorating electric transmission grid results in the loss of more than 30% of the energy. A national infrastructure program to address these weaknesses would result in millions of well-paid jobs both in construction and in manufacturing.

3. <u>Modernize the entire energy sector</u>: This starts with a modern and greatly expanded electric transmission grid to get <u>renewable</u> power from where it is best produced by solar, wind, tidal, geo-thermal, or fourth-generation, non-uranium, non-plutonium-based reactors that cannot experience a meltdown that releases radioactivity. Building these production facilities and the grid would generate millions more jobs in both construction and manufacturing, and potentially expand the tradeable goods sector as well. This would also slow climate change and the costs it imposes.

4. <u>Greatly expand and improve the educational system and revise its funding basis</u>:

- Professional, free childcare facilities for children under age 2 to allow single mothers to work and as a safety value for distressed families are urgently needed.
- The extraordinary benefits of universal, free, pre-school (age 2-4) education are well documented and urgently needed. (Some claim there is a payback of $12-$15 dollars for every $1 spent.)
- The standards for teacher credentialing and supervision for K-12 must be massively revised and

improved, and the salaries must be raised to attract the best and brightest young people. Who else should teach the children?

- The public university system must be seen as an extension of secondary education and provided at no or minimal direct cost to the students.

- The private colleges and universities, all of whom receive extensive public funding, must be required to educate a broad spectrum of the youth with matching public and private funding to enable those who qualify to attend, and to help qualify those who lack some preparation.

- The adult education system must be greatly expanded and upgraded to retrain workers for technologically demanding jobs in all sectors of the economy.

- The student loan program should be replaced with student financial aid grants and this money must be seen as an investment that is at least as important as that in infrastructure.

5.<u>Implement integrated community revitalization programs to help overcome the ravages of poverty and reduce crime.</u> Improving the future for poor children (which describes 20% of all U.S. children and almost 50% of minority kids) requires more than just better educational structures. It requires the development of a complex web of family and youth personal, career and college counseling and support services, anti-gang programs, community-based and focused law enforcement, a penal system that is refocused on rehabilitation and job training, and improved housing, recreational and transportation facilities - to name only the most obvious.

6. <u>A greatly expanded public-private partnership must be devoted to both basic and applied research.</u> This is needed to enrich and expand our tradable goods and services sector to bring down the trade deficit and to generate well-paying jobs.

7. <u>Funding the above six proposals</u>: The needed government money can only come from three possible sources: cuts in other government spending, higher taxes or more borrowing.

(a) <u>Cuts in Government Spending</u>: Over the span of eight years of the Bush Administration and five years of Obama, expenditures on all of the above types of programs have fallen, except during the 18-month period of the emergency stimulus program implemented at the beginning of Obama's term in response to the Great Recession he inherited. Non-military discretionary spending of the types enumerated above is now at its lowest levels as a percent of GDP in the last 35 years. Non-military, non-discretionary (also called mandatory) spending on programs such as Social Security, Medicare (for the elderly), and Medicaid (for the poor) has been expanding, but cannot responsibly be cut. This leaves only two places to get money: further cuts in military spending and reductions to the subsidies and tax-breaks (reductions) provided to businesses. Indeed, these two areas do provide a potential source of substantial funding. Military-related spending accounts for more than 60% of all discretionary spending. Tax breaks granted to businesses and individuals amount to more than all discretionary spending combined. The tax-breaks or tax reductions granted to business amount to more than half of the total. So there is indeed tens of billions of federal spending that could be put to better use.

(b) Taxes: There is a great deal of money, many billions of dollars, that can reasonably and appropriately be secured by a tax system that requires the rich and the near rich, and the corporations, including the banks and other financial institutions, to give back to their society a portion of what they have taken. [Note – I do not say "earned." All of these families and business have built their fortunes using the economic, political and social structures of the U.S. and then they do their best not to pay for these by never missing an opportunity to reduce the taxes they pay.] The nominal tax rate on corporations is 35%, but the effective tax rate is only 11% and many pay no taxes whatsoever. Similarly, the maximum marginal tax rate on upper class individuals and families is 36%, but most of them pay an average effective tax rate of 10-15%. In addition, a vast amount of business and private income and wealth is hidden abroad and must be brought back or at least taxed.

(c) Government Borrowing: Borrowing must be seen as an appropriate vehicle to spread the cost of long-term investments over the period of their

productivity. Government investments are not the same as government consumption – the buying of goods and services or the spending of money on
benefits that are used and gone at the end of the year. Government investments are expenditures that create assets that generate benefits over a long span of years. Money spent on infrastructure, education and research are such investments. These investments, as a matter of both economics and ethics, should not be paid in advance from tax dollars. The fact is that the rich and near rich and the corporations should be "encouraged" to view these loans to the government (i.e. these purchases of government bonds) as an appropriate vehicle to rebuild and improve their nation. Indeed, most of them will benefit greatly from such improvements. Therefore, they should not view the purchase of these government bonds (for which they will be paid interest) as an act of altruism, but rather as being in their own self-interest. After all, they themselves often borrow money to make long-term investments such as to build a new factory or create a new product. Why should they expect their government not to do the same?

As for the determination of the extent of responsible government annual deficits or of cumulative federal debt, these must be judged on the basis of the deficit or debt's cyclically adjusted percentage of GDP, not on the percentage of the government budget. On this basis, there is currently plenty of room for rather extensive borrowing. The deficit as a percentage of GDP has gone down during every year of the Obama administration from 10.1% in 2009 to 4.2% in 2013, and it is currently projected to drop to 2.3% by 2018. Given that the economy is still suffering from high unemployment and slow growth, doing the extra borrowing that would instead keep the deficit to GDP in the 3 to 5% range would not be the least bit irresponsible – especially if that money were going to the sort of investments enumerated in #1-6 above.

Finally: What are the Prospects that Any of these Proposals will be Implemented?

Here I cannot be optimistic at all. Making and sustaining long-term financial or policy commitments (other than military) is not something the U.S. government seems capable of doing. It used to be able to do this, witness the Eisenhower Administration's commitment to a 10-15 year program to build the interstate highway system. But today such a commitment seems politically impossible. Moreover, the ideological forces which are so insanely focused on lowering taxes, deficit reduction and cutting government spending, rather than on increasing social investment and employment, are hardly likely to be overcome by more rational forces. The rich and the corporations are not likely to allow their tax burden to be increased. Corporations will fight to prevent the needed adjustments in the labor market. The military-industrial-congressional complex (a term coined by

Eisenhower) will strongly resist further cuts to the military. And given these forces' increasing control over the political process, they are likely to win these struggles.

So the outlook is bleak. The U.S. economy (GDP) will grow, albeit at a far slower rate than could reasonably be expected, and unemployment will remain considerably higher and wages lower than need be. The labor force participation rate will continue to slip. The poor will continue to suffer; the middle class will continue to shrink and experience economic and social distress. Median household income will continue to stagnate. In short, while the corporations who profit from globalization will get stronger, and the rich richer, the rest of the economy will largely, and unnecessarily, stagnate. As Joe Nocera put it (New York Times, Jan 21, 2014) in an article unfavorably comparing U.S. fiscal policy to that of Brazil: "What's the point of economic growth if nobody has a job?" Or as Mark Shields (PBS Jan. 27, 2014) put it: "We must decide if people work for the economy or the economy works for the people." Sadly, these same questions must also be poised to the leaders of many European nations who are too focused on austerity, rather than on the growth of well-paying jobs.

This piece was also published in the May 2014 issue of the journal Streven: A Journal of Political Economy.

How Corporations Became People In The Eyes Of The Supreme Court (Issue #13)

By Merrill Ring

Many Americans have been deeply upset by the realization that our Supreme Court holds that corporations are persons. How could such an absurd proposition have become part of the American legal tradition? Here is the story.

To the best of my knowledge what I say here is correct, at least on the major points. Should I be mistaken I would be very pleased to learn the truth.

I shall summarize Thom Hartmann's account in his book *Unequal Protection*. Hartmann was not the first to have noticed many of the relevant points but he has the best overall non-academic presentation. On crucial points about the history as Hartmann presents it, I have not found any major criticisms (though there are several points of unclarity in his account.)

This story is both historically interesting and quite important as it should play some role in our attempt to overturn Citizen's United. To that end, I have sprinkled some pieces of my own commentary in the narrative.

Pre-14th Amendment

A distinction between *natural* and *artificial* persons – the latter being (at least chiefly) corporations – was originally worked out in English common law (the history of that development I don't know). The point of the distinction was to treat corporations as a kind of person in order to justify various matters pertaining to their legal status: as artificial persons they could own property, sign contracts, be taxed, sue and be sued in courts. The distinction between the two kinds of person was discussed in the authoritative commentary on the common law by William Blackstone published in the 18th century, a work known to the writers of the constitution and still cited by the Supreme Court in decisions. As the English common law became the basis of American law, we inherited that distinction.

If the notion of corporate personhood is abolished via constitutional amendment, the legal system will still have to have a means of recognizing the above features (e.g. property ownership) of the legal status of corporations – what is to be excluded by any constitutional amendment are only (only!) the right to *political speech* that the Citizens United decision gave corporations. However, it is a huge intellectual, and consequently political error, to base those legal rights (say to property ownership) on the claim that corporations are <u>any</u> kind of person (artificial persons) as the common law did and does. Following a future constitutional amendment, corporations should not be thought of as artificial persons but as some other kind of institutional entity.

14th Amendment

The 14th amendment (proposed by Congress in 1866, ratified by the states in 1868) provided equal protection of the law for all persons. The intent of this post-Civil War amendment was to wipe out legal distinctions between blacks and whites. However, the language of the amendment says merely "persons" not "natural persons" which, in light of the existing legal distinction between natural and artificial persons, it should have said to secure the intent of the amendment.

Not long after the amendment was accepted two Congressmen instrumental in writing the amendment, Senator Roscoe Conkling and Rep John Bingham, went on to become lawyers for the railroads - the major corporations in those days. Conkling bragged in a court case that it was they who had seen to it that the phrase "natural person" was not used in the 14th but only "person".

That language opened the door for corporations to argue that, since they were already a kind of person by common law, they were now entitled to equality with all other persons.

The 14th was passed hurriedly, with supporters admitting that they hadn't taken time to think through all the details. There was thus no Congressional discussion of whether the amendment concerned what had been known as 'artificial persons', i.e. corporations, no debate on whether the 14th was to give corporations equal protection under the law with living breathing American citizens. That legislative failure left it up to the law as to whether corporations were to be covered by the 14th.

1886: Southern Pacific Railroad v Santa Clara County

This was the crucial case that, according to legal scholars, established that, in light of the 14th amendment, corporations were persons and entitled to equal protection under the law with all other persons.

The case was a tax dispute that worked its way up to the Supreme Court. Southern Pacific's lawyers argued that Santa Clara County had wrongly taxed some railroad property. Their case had six different lines of argument. One of those arguments, carried on at some length, made appeal to the 14th amendment and claimed that the constitution had now made the railroad a person with consequences for the tax dispute.

The Court ruled for the railroad – but it did so on the narrow ground that the assessment of the property was conducted by the wrong agency. The decision said among much else: "These questions [regarding the 14th] belong to a class which this court should not decide unless their determination is essential to the disposal of the case.... Whether the present cases require a decision of them [the constitutional issues] depends upon the soundness of another proposition, upon which the court... in view of its conclusions upon other issues, did not deem it necessary to pass.... If these positions are tenable, there will be no occasion to consider the grave questions of constitutional law ... as the judgment can be sustained upon this ground, it is not necessary to consider any other questions raised by the pleading." *That is, the court did not consider the constitutional issue raised by the railroad*, and which was objected to by the defense, because it could find sufficient ground to come to a decision quite independently of the issues concerning the 14th amendment.

Thus the Court in the case that is thought to have established that corporations are persons did not consider the issue at all. Nonetheless it turns out that the entire American legal tradition thinks that the issue was discussed by the court in that case and decided in favor of corporate personhood.

The serious question comes up: how did that happen?

The Headnote

Hartmann considers some theories as to how it has come about that lawyers and judges believe that the 1886 case produced a decision that corporations were equally persons along with you and me. His own theory is this – and he argues it well.

The relevant decision (like all others) was published by the court reporter, one J.C. Bancroft Davis. At that time the court reporter was not a stenographer as she/he is today. Bancroft Davis was a significant political figure – he actually was paid more in his job than were any of the justices. At one time, 20 years previously, he had been on the board of directors of a railroad.

When he published the decision, he included in the publication what are called 'headnotes' –

commentary on the case by someone such as himself who had no part in the decision. Headnotes thus have no legal standing. In his headnote to this case Bancroft Davis wrote "One of the points made and discussed at length in the brief of counsel for defendants was that 'Corporations are persons within the meaning of the Fourteenth Amendment.... Before argument Mr. Chief Justice Waite said: 'The court does not wish to hear argument on the question whether the provision in the Fourteenth Amendment ... which forbids a State to deny to any person within its jurisdiction the equal protection of the laws, applies to these corporations. We are all of the opinion that it does."

Bancroft Davis' claim in the headnote that Chief Justice Waite said that his fellow justices agreed that corporations are persons is the source of the legal belief that the case settled that they are persons. By the time the decision was published (about 1½ years later) Waite was virtually dead and so he had no ability to see it. It is Hartmann's thesis that Bancroft Davis took it upon himself to include the comment in the headnote. The legal tradition has come to believe that the abstract (which is what a headnote amounts to) by Bancroft Davis of what the justices believed is what the decision said. But the court explicitly denied that the constitutional issue had a bearing on their decision.

Following the Southern Pacific case, corporations leaped to make use of the idea that the court had ruled that constitutionally they were full-fledged legal persons. Hartmann notes that the 14th amendment was not applied to women and to blacks until the 20th century – no matter what its language and intent – but corporations immediately began arguing on its basis over and over in cases affecting them. It was a corporate coup.

Harry Belafonte sang 'House built on a weak foundation will not stand.' The idea of corporate personhood as constitutionally guaranteed has been built on a phantom foundation – but it stands because it is enshrined in the American legal tradition, serving as precedent in so many Supreme Court rulings.

How Does The 14th Amendment Apply To The States? (Issue #5)

By Bob Gerecke

The 14th: is it about persons or about citizens? If the important clause is about citizens, then, since corporations are not citizens (even if the Supreme Court madly held them to be persons), they can be regulated by the states in ways that persons can't be.

Dean Erwin Chemerinsky may be correct that a Constitutional amendment is not necessary to counter the undemocratic effects of the Supreme Court's decision in *Citizens United.* The provision of the First Amendment which prohibits the Congress from abridging free speech may not apply to the States.

110

The 14th Amendment is usually cited as requiring the States to observe all of the guarantees of the U.S. Constitution. However, the section which is so interpreted doesn't exactly say that. Here's the text:

Section 1. All persons born or naturalized in the United States, and subject to the jurisdiction thereof, are citizens of the United States and of the State wherein they reside. No State shall make or enforce any law which shall abridge the privileges or immunities of citizens of the United States; nor shall any State deprive any person of life, liberty, or property, without due process of law; nor deny to any person within its jurisdiction the equal protection of the laws.

Notice that only citizens' – not persons' – "privileges and immunities" are protected from abridgment by the States. However, it is a person's "life, liberty and property" that are protected. The shift in wording from "citizens" to "person" cannot have been unintentional, and even if it was, it is a distinction in law.

An argument can be made that the states may limit free speech, a free press, and possession of firearms by non-citizens, and that corporations are surely non-citizens. Some state should pass a law to prohibit campaign contributions and expenditures by non-citizens in order to put the Supreme Court into a box: either interpret the 14th Amendment to say what

111

it says and not say what it doesn't say, or violate the conservatives' principle of interpreting the text only as written. If the Supreme Court protects the corporations, it will create a stir, confirm the impression that its majority is seeking a predetermined conclusion rather than an honest interpretation, and lend fuel to the movement for an amendment and for other legislation on the matter.

Conservatives will argue that denying some rights to non-citizens violates the final clause of the 14th Amendment, requiring "equal protection of the laws". However, that interpretation would throw other laws treating citizens and non-citizens differently into question, e.g., "illegal immigrant" laws and those requiring citizenship for an individual to vote in State elections and to make campaign contributions and political expenditures. It would be interesting to see if the Supreme Court could wiggle through this maze to obtain all of the results that its most conservative members want.

A Citizen's Response To The *Citizen's United* Decision (Issue #5)

By Merrill Ring

For someone not a legal professional (i.e. most of us), the Supreme Court's decision in Citizens United is madness and raises the question: How could they think that?

I'm not a lawyer or legal scholar. I think my reaction to the Supreme Court's decision in the *Citizens United* case is fairly typical of ordinary intelligent folk. Three matters have struck me and others, all leading to a lessening of the respect for the Court.

1. The idea that some members of the Supreme Court have treated and are treating Corporations as Persons strikes intelligent outsiders as plainly ludicrous. That comes out in the sign in the photo published in the vicinity of this essay: 'I'll Believe Corporations are Persons When Texas Executes One'. Another favorite of mine: one of the Latino geezers in the comic strip La Cucaracha declares that if corporations are persons he sure would like to date Victoria's Secret. We hear the Supremes talking of Corporations as Persons and we immediately think of what could happen to real persons – and that no corporation could possibly be subject to such things (being executed, having a hot date with, serving in the military, voting, being mayor or dog catcher, having a doctor's appointment, snoring....)

Now it may be that in certain respects corporations resemble persons – but so does my dog and she certainly more so than a corporation. But the Supremes have not held that as a constitutional matter dogs are persons. So why have they taken it as a matter of legal right that corporations should be treated in American law as persons? We outsiders think that no matter what the resemblance in this or that respect of a

113

corporation to a person there is nothing that could reasonably lead an intelligent and unbiased person to declare them to be people with the full set of rights and responsibilities of an American person. The conclusion must be that the Supremes' education and intelligence have been overwhelmed by some form of prejudice.

2. The decision involves calling and treating Money as Speech: and as we are prohibited from restricting speech in this country so we are prohibited from restraining the use of money in speaking (politically). Now it is true, as we all know, that money talks. But talking money is precisely what runs counter to democratic ideals which assume basic political equality. If we allow Money to be Speech, as the Court does, we undermine our democratic ideals. For if you have $1000 and I have $1, then you have the legal right to be 999 times more important in the political process than I am. It is not that you are (necessarily) superior to me in intelligence, education, concern, knowledge, wisdom and therefore you should be listened to more than me. It is just that you have a lot more money than me and that money can be freely used to push your political views without regard to the important distinctions between people that make one person's views better than another's.

Money is not Speech – it is a medium of exchange that enables persons to do or purchase things they desire. When what is done or purchased is a political privilege, that is a point of concern for those addicted to democracy, a legitimate reason for legal restraints on the use of money to affect political decisions. It is shocking to ordinary people that persons as intelligent and as educated as the Justices of the Supreme Court declare that money should freely talk and talk extremely loudly in our democracy, in effect rendering it formally a plutocracy.

3. If it is objected that the *Citizen's United* decision is merely the latest in a line of decisions treating Corporations as Persons and treating Money as Speech and hence those precedents mean the court is correct in reaching the conclusion that it did in the most recent case, we outsiders can only think that that is a mad view of the role of precedent in normal human life and even in legal decisions. Surely those who made the original decision were people and so subject to error. To argue that the Court must have come to the conclusions that it did in *Citizen's* because it has been written in stone that Corporations are Persons and that Money is Speech strikes us legal outsiders as madness. The lemming who leaps because all those who preceded him/her have leaped should not be the principle of human life and of legal decisions. Try this principle: Think! Emerson said that consistency was the virtue of small minds: to encourage the above kind of respect to precedent reveals nothing but a small (or lemming) mind. The poem goes 'Oh what a tangled web we weave when first we practice to deceive.' The same goes when we blindly follow the mistakes others have made in pursuit of nothing other than consistency.

Obama Embraces Chump Economics (Issue #16)

By Ivan Light

Romney might well have lied and stimulated the economy via military Keynesianism while Obama might (sadly) keep his word and forego an equivalent but productive program of expenditures

During the political campaign, Romney claimed that he could create more jobs than could President Obama. Mostly we just scoffed, but ask yourself: how might his claim have proven correct? The answer hinges on Romney's cryptic five-point plan, details of which he refused to disclose. Romney said that he would add two trillion dollars to the defense budget, reduce tax receipts by five trillion dollars, and nonetheless balance the budget. Obama replied that Romney's plan could not work because Romney could not increase expenditures, reduce taxes, and balance the budget without drastically cutting social security and Medicare, which Romney declared he would "never" do. Romney promised a fiscal miracle that he could not deliver. Romney was selling snake oil. Obama was right about that.

However, Romney's plan was only snake oil if Romney meant what Romney said. What if Romney lied to the voters? Suppose Romney did not really care about balancing the federal budget, and just claimed to care in order to conform his stated policy with the

GOP's platform; however, suppose further that Romney intended all along to forget deficit reduction as soon as he was elected President. This is what George W. Bush did. Possibly Romney took a play from Bush's book, and that play *might have worked.*

By cutting taxes on the wealthy, Romney would have stimulated spending to some modest extent, and the result would be enhanced job creation. By throwing unnecessary money at the Pentagon, thus increasing the federal deficit, Romney would also create employment. Taking both policies together, Romney's plan would indeed create employment just as he promised, but it would have increased federal debt. Under Romney, the federal budget deficit would have hugely increased, but his policies would have increased employment all right. The main beneficiaries of Romney's largesse would have been the rich and the Defense Department, two core constituencies of the Republican Party, but some economic benefit would have trickled down to Joe Six Pack. The unsolved problem would have been, of course, the vast increase in government deficit which this policy of "military Keynesianism" would have produced. Military Keynesianism is the policy of stimulating the economy by reckless and unnecessary spending on defense.

But would anyone really care in 2016 that Romney increased the deficit if he reduced unemployment? I don't care now, and neither did Richard M. Nixon back in 1972 nor do progressive economists like Paul Krugman, and I suspect that

Romney does not care either. The truth is only chumps care about deficits during deep recessions. Romney is not a chump. Once elected, Romney might well have forgotten his deficit reduction pledge, and taken credit for increasing employment. He would claim to have accomplished this feat by successful restructuring of the private sector, cutting "red tape," getting tough with the Chinese, etc. But the real reason would have been military Keynesianism. Voters would forget and forgive the increase in the deficit out of gratitude for the increase in employment, and reelect Romney in 2016.

Well, Romney lost, so what now? It's not over. Unlike Romney, President Obama actually feels obliged to reduce the federal deficit as Bill Clinton did. Obama promised to do so, and, unfortunately, he meant it. This promise, which, unlike Romney, President Obama takes seriously, now compels Obama to reduce government spending and to increase taxes on the rich. That's how deficits get reduced. However, those two policies in tandem tend to reduce employment. It is easy to increase employment by lowering taxes and deficit spending; hard to do it while reducing government spending and raising taxes.

The fact is, alas, Obama's misguided fidelity to the deficit reduction credo has already created problems for the economy, and now creates them anew for the future. By following a conservative economic policy of austerity, the first Obama administration forsook what should have been a Democratic administration's main program tool for stimulating employment: vigorous counter – cyclical spending that increased federal deficits while rebuilding our civilian infrastructure and setting up the green economy that will carry the USA through the next fifty years. The result of Obama's "highly responsible policy" of austerity was a feeble recovery that permitted the Republicans to complain that they could produce more jobs.

It need not have been this way. Had Obama embraced Franklin Roosevelt's policy of massive government spending to create employment, as the progressive wing of his own party begged him to do, then Obama might have greatly strengthened the economy's job creation. In that case, Republicans could not have complained with as they did with some justice that the recovery has been anemic. Instead, Obama embraced austerity, and got the feeble growth austerity permits. In effect, Obama embraced a conservative economic nostrum, austerity, and meant it, whereas the Republicans have secretly taken on board military Keynesianism.

Duplicity is the key to Republican economic policy. Sure, their arithmetic makes no sense, but who cares about that? When challenged to get real during the debate, Romney and Ryan issued bald face lies about their devotion to deficit reduction, and declared the existence of secret plans whose arithmetic implied the stimulation of the economy by increasing (not reducing) the deficit.

Now that Obama has been reelected on a deficit-reduction plank, progressives must fear that he will actually adhere to the unsound economic policy on which he ran. If he does that, and thus sabotages the nation's chances for economic growth in the next four years, then in 2016 Republicans will be able justly to claim that his economic policy failed eight years in a row. *They will be right* because Obama accepted a "responsible" economic policy that rightly belonged in the Republican platform whereas the Republicans duplicitously embraced military Keynesianism. Austerity economics do not work any better when Democrats introduce them.

One may say, in extenuation, that at least Obama was honest about what he intended to do whereas the Republicans lied. Alas, that would make a very sad epitaph for the Democratic Party's tombstone. The way forward is for Obama to forget about the deficit, and rebuild the civilian infrastructure of the United States at federal government expense while also setting up a high-tech green economy that can compete with Germany and China despite their advantage in those fields at this time. In 2016 Republicans will then say, hey, Obama increased the deficit! But no one will care because the country will be enjoying prosperity, and looking at a rosy future.

Back to Class Warfare: The Rhetoric of Mitt Romney (Issue #15)

By David Depew

The undeserving poor, the biggest group in the 47%, are the creatures of a 19th century picture of classes and class warfare!

As Marx predicted, capitalism collapsed and weak liberal democratic governments collapsed with it. This happened in the 1930s. After World War II Humpty Dumpty was put back together again in a way that rendered the notion of class conflict, which had been on everyone's tongues for decades, rhetorically inaccessible in political discourse. Everyone began to identify as middle class. The previously marginalized American right wing rose to its current prominence because Ronald Reagan relentlessly engaged in happy talk about the benefits to all of transferring wealth to the already wealthy. It would be morning in America. The Bushes echoed him.

What is striking about Mitt Romney is that he is utterly deaf to these rhetorical pieties. He lives in a 19th century political imaginary. There are for him, as there were then, two kinds of poor, the deserving and the undeserving. In America, Romney claims, about 5% of the population falls into the first class, the deserving poor. This problem will never go away so there is no need to try to make it go away. "The poor you will always with you," said Jesus (Matthew 26: 11), suggesting that he might not have considered himself poor, presumably because he could always build houses or go fishing with his disciples to turn a drachma. If the system of poor relief (as it was called in

121

Dickensian times) needs fixing, Romney says he will fix it. He envisions, it seems, a mix of private, largely religious, and public assistance on the basis of demonstrated dire straits.

The undeserving poor, by contrast, are in Romney's world what used to be called "able bodied men" who shirk their responsibilities. Romney suspects they think of themselves the way Elisa Doolittle's father did in *My Fair Lady*: as a "victim of middle class morality", a morality that has a ridiculous insistence on the Protestant work ethic and Victorian chastity.

This 42% (the 47% less the deserving poor) lumps together an assorted lot. One chunk of the 42% are working families with children who pay no federal income tax—they pay plenty of other taxes, many regressive—because their salaries are too small to be taxable. How did this happen? Easy. Congressmen of both parties collaborated to create Earned Income Tax Credits and other such programs because they wanted to bring home the bacon but were afraid to implicate themselves in raising tax *rates*.

Another chunk of the 42% are retired people. Since he considers Medicare and Social Security a form of the dole, Romney has lowered his own cognitive dissonance by imagining that recipients of these programs, who have paid into them all their working lives, consider themselves entitled to these goodies because, like Elisa Doolittle's dad, they have been victimized.

What about the 53%? Except among the famous 1% in which Romney himself lives, moves, and has his being—beneficiaries of the same kind of finance capitalism that did in the world economy in the 1930s-- they are in Romney's mind the good old entrepreneurial American middle class who built this country in the days before the post War consensus institutionalized New Deal and Great Society thinking. That old middle class, he thinks, will re-build the country again - but only when he and other conservatives have fully rolled back Roosevelt's and Johnson's handiwork.

This rollback they intend to do. If Romney thinks that the 47% will never vote for him, it is because he imputes to them an implausibly high degree of awareness of what he is up to. Not for Romney the conventional wisdom that the American working class votes against its own interests because it mistakenly believes that the oligarchs support its moral issues. No, for Romney the 47% can count as well as he can and figure they will make out like bandits under the Democrats.

The math is interesting here too. Oddly, Romney uses the $250,000 mark at which President Obama proposes to steepen the marginal tax rate as a class demarcator. (Obama, whose rhetoric draws on the conventional myth that we all are or, with the right public policies, might all be in the same class, does not use the figure as a upper boundary of the middle class.) "Middle income is $200,000 to $250,000 and less," Romney told George Stephanopolous. But not *much* less. In saying this he was explicitly denying Stephanopoulos's surmise that he was thinking of $100,000 as middle income.

This way of figuring class membership certainly reflects Romney's personal situation as a beneficiary of finance capitalism. He made $14,000,000 in 2011 without lifting a finger, so $200,000 must look pretty cheesy to him. But it is also consistent with writing off 47% of the population as morally corrupted by the New Deal. If the enterprising middle class settles around $200,000 it is easy to find 47% who, because they make at most a measly $100,000, might, to Mitt's mind, feel aggrieved by the very existence of people like himself and so might feel entitled to grab everything they can get from the government.

In short, Romney imagines the 47% as envious and resentful. In the real world, however, it just so happens that median family income is about $50,000. People in this income range are not salaried but hourly workers. But, as interviews with Barbara Ehrenreich show, many people in this situation reveal, by their palpable fear of falling out of it, a solidly middle class sense of self. Some might feel aggrieved or entitled. After all, they are constantly being nickeled and dimed, as Ehrenreich puts it. But most feel grateful what whatever help they get to stay out of the pit of poverty by getting what work, health care, child support, skills training, tuition tax credits, and food stamps they can. It was on the perception that you can separate the cheaters and chisellers, who no doubt do exist, from people who want to work but need help that Bill Clinton's more or less successful reform of the work/welfare relation was predicated.

Where, then, are Romney's resentful 47%? Mostly, I think, in his head. If Romney sounds like the Man From The 19th Century it is because he is. He sees the political and social landscape in terms of class interest, class identity, and class conflict.

It is often said that this is an important election. This perception has to do with more than who will control Congress and the Supreme Court, important as these are. It is about what will happen now that the shared fiction about class harmony that Reagan co-opted from FDR has worn thin enough to see through. If you want to know what the landscape will look like after the election, I suggest you get your fill of American political speeches and punditry from the 1880s to about 1940. No matter who wins in 2012, you will be taking yourself back to the future.

This article will be re-published later in POROI: An Interdisciplinary e-journal of Rhetorical Analysis and Invention, Vol 8, number 2

Equality, Industrial Capitalism, the Declaration and the Constitution (Issue #22)

By Merrill Ring

Where in the Declaration of Independence and the Constitution is the relation between human equality and wealth confronted?

The new style 'conservatives', given their commitment to freedom as the sole political value, read the Declaration of Independence as nothing more than an assertion of freedom.

What they ignore is that while the Declaration announces and justifies the claimed freedom of the colonies from British rule, it does not otherwise treat freedom as the sole, not even the major, value for the people of the colonies.

The Declaration opens with a brief paragraph noting that the colonies were in this document declaring themselves free from the political bonds that tied them to Britain. It goes on to say that an explanation and defense of breaking away from its mother country is needed. In the 2nd paragraph, the Declaration begins that explanation.

It opens with words familiar to Americans: "We hold these truths to be self-evident, that all men are created equal...." What is so widely overlooked, especially by conservatives espousing freedom in every aspect of life, is that when the time comes to defend the act of declaring political freedom, the very first thing that is said in that defense rests upon the natural equality of all men. It is implied that remaining under British rule would not allow the colonists to achieve the natural state of equality with each other and with others. Hence independence, self-rule, is declared.

What form of political life is suitable for a people committed to idea that all men are created equal? After reflection and experience, it was realized (more or less widely) that democracy is the system best suited to that starting point.

It took more than a decade that included a war to achieve independence and a failed try at a workable political arrangement before the founders established a Constitution that satisfied them as roughly meeting the requirement that everyone be thought of as equal. It is not easy, however, to be clear and certain what constitutes the translation of the fundamental thought that all men are created equal into practical, democratic terms. Only slowly did we come to see that more was required than the founders realized. Slavery had to be overcome – women had to acquire political rights – and several other developments were necessary (and there are other conditions that have not yet been realized in practice.) In short, we did not become a full democracy with the creation and acceptance of the Constitution.

In the attempt to express constitutionally the thought that we are equal, there was an issue over and above the failure to confront slavery and the place of women that largely escaped the founders. What should be done about the role of wealth in a democracy?

No doubt the founders did not deeply consider

that problem for several reasons. They themselves were men of wealth and since they were trying to set out what makes for the common good, they assumed that wealth was not a major issue for a democratic government.

More importantly, wealth at that time was largely in land ownership. The wealthy owned land and the tools to work it – the poor did not. What they did not realize was that at the same time as we were becoming a country, there was a major change in the economic life of England and soon elsewhere. A new form of capitalism, industrial capitalism, was just getting underway in Britain. The nature of capitalism itself was not understood – the first great explanation of that type of economy – Adam Smith's The Wealth of Nations - was published in 1776, the same year as the Declaration of Independence.

Our founders had substantial knowledge about and interest in political theory and political history, but they had no glimmer of modern economic life. There is thus nothing to be found in our Constitution about the economic system that was springing up in Britain and no thought given to the possibility that the great wealth created by modern capitalism would cause problems for the asserted equality of men and the democratic form of government that was being created to achieve that equality.

Thus we today cannot look to the founders and to our basic political document for guidance on how to maintain the fundamental assumption that we are equal. And it is surely obvious that from the Gilded Age (say 1890 to 1933) that vastly increasing wealth, and the power it confers, has been the chief tension in our political and economic lives. Today we have reached a state of inequality among our citizens that rivals that of the Gilded Age, undermining the assertion of the Declaration of Independence that all men are created equal. That circumstance was temporarily improved by the election of FDR in 1932. But the resurgence of the plutocrats beginning about 1970 has overwhelmed that attempt to re-establish equality as a fundamental value of the country. The talk these days is about how far the country has lost its democratic character and become instead an oligarchy, a plutocracy. The next several years will make that the basic issue of our political lives.

An Overview of the U.S. Occupy (Wall Street) Movement (Issue #10)

By Andy Winnick

I have been asked to write an article that provides for a European audience an overview of the Occupy Movement in the U.S. – no small task, and one I take on with a deep sense of humility, for this is a broad, somewhat amorphous, and still emerging and developing social phenomenon.

The Origins of the U.S. Occupy Movement

Ironically, the U. S. Occupy Wall Street (often referred to as OWS) movement has its origins abroad. The events of the Arab Spring and the Spanish *Indignados* movement, which began in Madrid in May 2011, had begun to spur discussions among progressives in the U.S. as to why similar demonstrations had not begun in the U.S. We observed the widespread economic distress that had followed the financial crisis of December 2007 and was continuing for millions of Americans despite what was formally called a recovery (which technically began in July 2009) and we wondered why so little outrage. We understood that since the 1970's, the American middle class had been under increasing economic pressure, with the distribution of income growing steadily more inequitable, especially since the 1980s. Academics had written books and hundreds of articles about this, but with little political or public effect.

Then, on July 13, 2011, the Vancouver, Canada-based, anti-consumerism Adbusters Media Foundation created the Twitter hash tag #OCCUPYWALLSTREET and via Twitter and emails sent out the proposal to begin a demonstration in New York City on September 17th (U.S. Constitution Day) to express outrage over "the growing disparity in wealth and the absence of legal repercussions for the bankers behind the recent global financial crisis." Via emails and social networks, with the hackers group Anonymous jumping in to help, the idea spread quickly. And on the day suggested, in Zuccotti Park near Wall Street in New York City, the

Occupy Wall Street movement began its encampment and demonstrations. (This site was chosen because it was a privately owned public space and not subject to the city's curfew policy for public parks.) Immediately, regular marches from the park to Wall Street began, with demonstrations in front of various financial institutions. While there was some media attention, it was initially quite muted and limited.

Nevertheless, what was amazing was that within weeks, similar Occupy demonstrations and encampments sprang up in more than 800 cities in the U.S. spurred on by communications via the Internet. Virtually instantaneously, the tent became Occupy's symbolic form of free speech, the symbol of their determination to stay in place until change occurred. By January 2012, only four months from its beginning, there were (and in many cases still are) Occupy efforts in more than 1400 U.S. cities, including in at least 59 California cities. Also, within a month or two of the initial OWS effort in September 2011, there were Occupy demonstrations in at least 135 cities in 35 European nations, including 17 cities in England, plus others in 32 cities in 16 Latin American countries and others in 14 Asian nations. By mid-January 2012, the Occupy movement identified efforts in 2,773 communities across the world. This had truly become a global phenomenon.

One does need to acknowledge immediately that the OWS movement cannot and does not "claim credit" for most of the European efforts. Clearly, as noted, some of these (Spain in particular) preceded and inspired OWS. The austerity programs initiated by the British government clearly provoked many demonstrations in the UK long before OWS emerged. Nevertheless, many of the demonstrations in Europe since September 2011 took on the title and tactics of the OWS movement, chose to label themselves with the "Occupy" designation, and adopted the "We are the 99%" slogan.

The Phrase "We are the 99%"

The awareness of the growing disparity in income and wealth between the richest 1% of Americans and the other 99% certainly did not gain notoriety only with the Occupy movement in the fall of 2011. Many books and articles had been written about this for years. The issue was raised as far back as 1987 in a book by Professor Batra of SMU (*The Great Depression of 1990*) that was #1 on the New York Times best seller list, and in a book I published in 1989, entitled *Toward Two Societies: The Changing Distributions of Income and Wealth in the U.S.* In the 2000 Presidential elections, Al Gore accused George W. Bush of supporting "the wealthiest 1%." There was a documentary film entitled *The One Percent* by Jamie Johnson in 2006. In May 2011, Joseph Stiglitz, the Nobel prize-winning economist, published the article "Of the 1%, by the 1%, for the 1%" in *Vanity Fair* magazine. But then, in August 2011, an "anonymous 28-year-old New York activist named 'Chris'" launched a *Tumblr* blog with the title "We are the 99%" and this instantly became the political rallying cry of the Occupy Wall Street movement.

The facts validating the concern over the growing gap between the 1% and the 99% are well known. According to official U.S. government data, the richest 1% held a peak proportion of U.S. income of 23.9% in 1928. This proportion then fell rather steadily to only 9.1% by 1980. But then, starting with the Reagan Administration, the proportion increased again to reach 23.5% in 2007, before pulling back a bit with the financial crisis. Indeed, the Congressional Budget Office, a respected non-partisan agency, reported that from 1979 to 2007, the income of the top 1% increased by 275% while that of the poorest 20% increased by only 18%. During the same time period, the average pre-tax income of the bottom 90% actually decreased by $900, while that of the top 1% increased by more than $700,000. The after-tax proportions were even more striking as the income tax rates paid by the richest Americans fell steadily from 1980 to the present. In fact, Obama is the first U.S. President in more than 30 years to propose raising the taxes on the very rich.

According to the most recent Commerce Department figures, the share of income produced in the U.S. that is flowing to workers as salary and wages has been steadily shrinking since the mid-1970s and is now the lowest since record-keeping began in 1947.

Moreover, both public and private agency studies (including work by the OECD) have confirmed that inter-generational income mobility has slowed greatly in the U.S. and now lags that in many European nations. That is, it is growing less likely that someone born into one of the lower income categories will move into a higher one as a result of their own efforts and circumstances. In addition, recent opinion polls in the U.S. have revealed that for the first time ever, the current generation does not expect its children to lead a better life. So, not only has the extent of inequality (which, of course, many think is unfair) gotten much worse, the hopes of the American people that "things will get better" for their children have dimmed. In fact, in a January 2012 study by Charles Murray (*Coming Apart: The State of White America: 1960-2010),* it is argued that, even setting aside racial and ethnic differences, a new mammoth cultural and economic gap has emerged since the 1960's between the top 20% and the bottom 30% that is unlike anything that has occurred in the U.S. before. This study confirms and expands upon a trend I wrote about in 1989, reflected in the title of my book (mentioned above) *Toward Two Societies...*

The point is that the facts have been well documented for a long time, but it was not until the Occupy Wall Street movement took up the issue and chose, brilliantly in my view, to identify themselves with the slogan "We are the 99%," that the issue really captured the public's attention. By choosing this slogan, OWS avoided the divisiveness of pitting the poor and working classes against the middle class and avoided ethnic and gender divisions. They chose a unifying slogan that allowed the majority of Americans to feel that the OWS movement was speaking on their behalf.

Who are the Occupy Movement Demonstrators?

From my own observations, and from many articles about and videos and pictures of the demonstrators, a pretty clear picture begins to emerge. To understand who is participating, it is important to note that while large groups of people have been involved in the actual encampments in cities across the U.S., the demonstrators regularly leave their encampments to march in protest to key sites: city halls, large banks and other financial institutions, the U.S. Congress, etc. For example, demonstrations occurred on January 17 (the four-month anniversary) at each of the eleven Federal Reserve System regional bank headquarters. These marches attract many who cannot or will not engage in the encampments themselves, but who nevertheless clearly want to demonstrate their identification with the Occupy Movement, and with the slogan, "We are the 99%." (It should be noted that in other cities, the movement takes on the name of the local site: Occupy L.A., Occupy Cleveland, Occupy (Washington) D.C., etc.

So who are these demonstrators, many of whom are also staying at the encampments for various lengths of time? While they are primarily young, mid-teens to early 30s, in fact observations and pictures show many with gray hair, including many who are clearly quite old. In interviews with these various demonstrators, one soon hears the voices and sees the faces of:

- young recent college graduates who cannot find work in their professions, or often cannot find any work at all
- college graduates who are overwhelmed by student loans that they cannot repay because they are either unemployed or earn too little to make the payments and survive.
- high school graduates who cannot afford to go to college and who cannot find work
- retirees who have lost their life savings and cannot survive on Social Security, and who often have lost their homes in the housing crisis
- working people who lost their jobs and are unemployed, or who have found work but at less than half what they had earned before, and as a result may have lost their homes
- couples who are working at such low wages that even with two full-time salaries they cannot earn much more than the poverty level of income, and again may have lost their homes
- veterans of the Iraq or Afghanistan wars who cannot find work
- school teachers, all with Bachelor's degrees, many with Master's degrees, who have been laid off as the money to support education has been cut back drastically because of budget crises at the state and local levels
- other public employees who have similarly

been laid off, and again many of these people have either lost their homes or are about to

- construction workers who have in many cases not worked since the housing industry collapsed some four years ago. (Why build new houses when millions are on sale as foreclosures at a fraction of the price they originally sold for?)
- workers who built or installed carpets, household appliances, roofing materials, or plumbing fixtures, but who are unemployed since there is no demand for these products or services since new housing construction is at the lowest level since World War II
- auto and steel workers who are either unemployed, or who have been re-hired but at wages about half what they earned before being laid off – and who now cannot afford the payments on their homes
- occasionally, small business owners who have suffered during this economic crisis and whose once reliable ties to banking institutions (for small business loans) have collapsed, even as those banks (which caused the crisis) were bailed out by the government
- a surprisingly large number of people who have not been particularly impacted by the financial crisis, but who are very upset by the growing inequity in the distribution of income and of political power

- and finally, in many cities, officials and rank and file labor movement members who recognize in the Occupy Movement allies in the labor movement's own on-going struggle for the interests of working people.

The list goes on and on describing a broad cross-section of the American public, across all ethnic lines, and from both big city and small town America. These encampments and demonstrations truly do encompass much of the 99% of the American people. In fact, this broad participation in the Occupy movement is a testament to the accuracy and relevance of the "We are the 99%" slogan," and at the same time is proof of its widespread appeal.

An interesting sidelight of this phenomenon is to watch the reaction of U.S. politicians. Most of those in the U.S. Senate and many in the U.S. House of Representatives are clearly in the 1%, many in the top 0.1%. Some react by objecting to the slogan as un-American class warfare; some simply ignore their own income level and say they support the 99%; others, including Obama, concede that they are in the 1% (in his case due to the royalties from his books), but make it clear that they support the analysis and goals of the Occupy movement and the 99%. But since September 2011, none of them can any longer ignore this divide.

Who are the 1%, and Is The More Relevant Issue Who are Those in the Top 0.1% of the Income Distribution?
When one hears the term "the richest 1%," the

inclination is to immediately think of millionaires, even billionaires, in terms of wealth and/or income. But that is not factually correct. To be in the top 1% of income recipients in the U.S. in 2009 took less than $350,000 in income. (It is estimated that at the moment, early 2012, it takes a bit more, $380,000, to qualify.) On the other hand, while that was the minimum in 2009, the average income of the 1.4 million households in this group then was $960,000; that is, just under the $1 million mark. This threshold changes every year, primarily due to changes in the stock, bond and various secondary markets where these folks hold much of their wealth and from which they derive much of their income. But what is even more interesting is who these 1%ers are. Financial professionals (the bankers, hedge fund managers, stock brokers, etc.) make up only about 14% of this group, while executives, managers and supervisors outside the financial industry make up more than twice this proportion, 31%. Interestingly, medical professionals make up another 16%, while lawyers constitute about 8%. That leaves 31% to be found scattered among the rest of the occupational categories.

It turns out that the really influential group is the top **0.1%,** not 'merely' the top **1%.** These 150,000 households earn a minimum of around $1.6 million per year; while a yet wealthier group, the top **0.01%,** have minimum incomes of $5.5 million and account for about 11,000 households. It is really the latter who can afford to give campaign contributions of millions of dollars, often tens of millions, emboldened by recent

Supreme Court decisions that for the first time allow for unlimited contributions. This is happening in the Republican Presidential primary campaign now underway.

What are the Goals of the Occupy Movement?

One keeps hearing the questions: But what do they really want? What are their goals? What do they expect the 1% to do? What do they really think the political establishment and political institutions can or should do? How can they expect to achieve much of anything if they do not present a clear list of well thought-out demands? Given the breadth, depth and diversity of people who identify with the Occupy movement these are not easy questions to answer, but in fact the answers are there and are really quite discernible.

First, in looking for the Occupy movement's goals or demands, the issue is where to look, to whom to talk, what to read. The point is that a foundational element of the Occupy movement is its structure, in particular its decision-making structure. A key element of the movement is its commitment to grassroots, participatory democracy and its sincere and deep-seated aversion to the identification of visible leaders or spokespersons. At each of the Occupy encampments, the only decision making-body is the General Assembly, whose meeting time and place is very publicly announced in advance. This group consists of whoever shows up. Everyone has equal rights to speak, and having any one individual dominate a discussion is not tolerated. Civility of discourse is a priority and to this end they have developed a series of silent hand gestures that are used when seeking to speak (these run from a simple request to talk, to a desire to directly respond to a previous point, to seek to clarify a point, or to raise a point of order) or when expressing one's views on an issue (including hand signals for agreement, simply not agreeing, strongly opposing, or being willing to try to block an action). Use of these hand signals is a way to prevent shouting and yelling out and to encourage civil discourse, while still being focused on reaching a consensus when possible, or at least a strong majority, on a given decision.

Media and other observers who come to an encampment or to a meeting of its General Assembly are encouraged to talk to whomever is there: typically no one is designated as "the spokesperson" and certainly not as "the leader." (There is sometimes a "media group" that is designated to interact with reporters on a particular day.) Nevertheless, each group makes clear decisions as to the site of a demonstration, what key slogans to emphasize, what points need to be made to those encountered along the way or at the demonstration site. While some strong personalities can often be identified at a given site at a given time, and these may be sought out by the media for their comments, the movement has been remarkably able to prevent the emergence of visible leadership *per se.* Many in the movement have indicated that this is a conscious reflection of the desire to maintain their broad base and broad appeal and to live the ideal of being "we the people" in the democratic sense in which that term was used in the U.S. Constitution.

Moving from the issue of process within the movement to an examination of its goals, one of the movement's influential members (Robert Jensen, a professor at the University of Texas in Austin) has stated:

"There's one question that pundits and politicians keep posing to the Occupy gatherings around the country: What are your demands? I have a suggestion for a response: We demand that you stop demanding a list of demands. The demand for demands is an attempt to shoehorn the Occupy gatherings into conventional politics, to force the energy of these gatherings into a form that people in power recognize, so that they can roll out strategies to divert, co-opt, buy off, or – if those tactics fail – squash any challenge to business as usual."

Instead, Jensen urges the movement to focus on sharpening its understanding that the problems that stem from the concentration of wealth and power in the U.S. have to be understood as being systemic in nature, and not simply the result of some group of corrupt or greedy corporate executives or politicians. His overarching point is that issuing demands while the current political-economic system remains in place is a useless exercise. Even more useless is to demand a change in personnel within the system, while leaving the system intact, since others who would be subject to the same political-economic pressures and values would quickly replace them.

More broadly, at every Occupy site one hears the clear message that the overarching systemic change that must be wrought is to severely limit the influence of the rich and powerful and of major financial and other corporations on American society, on its government at all levels, on its cultural, educational, political, journalistic and other institutions. There is a growing awareness throughout the U.S. that a series of recent Supreme Court decisions (the best known of which is the *Citizens United* decision in January 2010) have established that money is an expression of free speech, that corporations and the rich can use unlimited amounts of their own money to influence elections, and that it is permissible to keep secret the sources of massive contributions of money used to support electoral campaigns. The Occupy movement around the country has often joined voices with many others to call for a constitutional amendment to overturn these decisions. (For example, official resolutions to this effect have been passed by city councils in New York and Los Angeles and even by states such as Montana -- and are pending in many other jurisdictions.)

Balancing the emphasis on severely limiting the

influence of the rich is the clearly and often expressed desire to re-focus society's institutions on addressing the needs of the 99%. Particular emphasis is put on the need to end, indeed to reverse, the terrible housing foreclosure process that has driven literally millions of American families out of their homes in the last 3 or 4 years. At virtually every Occupy demonstration there are calls to force the banks to renegotiate people's home mortgages to reflect the drop in housing prices (of 40% or more since 2008) and to reduce the interest rates (to the current level of under 4%).

But beyond these specific issues, the Occupy movement reflects a growing awareness that the political economic system in the U.S. is fundamentally broken (as seems true in many other nations as well), and that the recent financial crisis (of December 2007 through 2009 in the U.S. – and on-going in Europe) is something much more than just another in a long list of periodic crises and recessions. Rather one hears more understanding that the shift toward a growing middle class and a shrinking gap between rich and poor in the U.S. which had occurred from 1945 to the mid-1970's has been reversed since then. Instead, the gap has been widening for more than 35 years, during which time the wealthiest elements in American society have steadily undermined the sense that there is an effective, functioning democracy. So the concerns of the Occupy movement go far beyond calling for a list of specific, marginal changes within the current structure of American society, rather what is being sought is a major restructuring.

Some (Jensen, Bayer) have suggested that those structural changes which the Occupy movement seeks can be grouped into three topic areas: **economics, empire, and ecology.** Under **economics**, it is argued that it is not merely the distributions of income and wealth that need to change, but rather it is the underlying capitalist economic structure that has generated those distributions, and will always tend to do so, that needs to be changed. It is not that economic markets and private property are not a viable form of organization: Occupy is not a socialist movement. Rather, the Occupy movement argues that those markets must be closely and continuously monitored and regulated in the interests of the 99%. Occupy contends that taxes and government spending must support the needs of the 99%, especially in the areas of housing (particularly forcing the renegotiation of many mortgages to end many of the foreclosures and to provide housing for the homeless), education (including colleges), healthcare, the improvement of the public infrastructure, and also support for small businesses which employ the majority of workers and whose owners are also part of the 99%. We can see how difficult waging this argument will be as the topic begins to be debated in the current Presidential campaign. The Republican party takes as its central focus attacking President Obama for the steps he has taken to pursue some modest regulation of the financial sector, stronger enforcement of environmental and product safely regulations, and slightly higher taxes on the rich and corporations. He is accused of waging "un-American class warfare," being "anti-American and anti-capitalist," and of wanting to move America to be more like the "failed socialist nations of Europe."

The focus on **empire** is revealed in the many signs and comments that state the need for the U.S. to withdraw from its empire and use the money for "nation building" at home, to stop viewing itself as the self-appointed policeman of the world, and to resist the claim of "American exceptionalism" in foreign policy generally.

On the **ecology / environmental** front, the Occupy demonstrators consistently support moving to green energy sources, environmentally safe production technologies and products, and efforts to reduce greenhouse gas emission and slow climate change.

For an example of the articulation of many of these, dare we say "demands," see the ***Declaration of the Occupy D.C.*** group which has been encamped in Washington, D.C. since October 1, 2011 and which adopted its statement on November 30, 2011. (http://occupydc.org/community/declaration/)

The Tactics of the Occupy Movement and Its Successes To-date

With a few rare exceptions, the Occupy movement has been committed to non-violent protest and demonstration, and to doing so in a legal manner. In most circumstances, the groups have not chosen the route of civil disobedience. There have been a few exceptions when the authorities sought to close encampments and move people out of them – but even in those circumstances, most Occupy groups and participants chose to leave peacefully and did not seek to be arrested. Oakland, California has sometimes been an exception to this pattern, in part due to harsh police tactics and the presence of some provocateurs. In every encampment and at every demonstration, all members of the public are invited to join in, visit, talk and even participate in the General Assemblies. The primary tactic, other than that of "occupying" public space (and occasionally foreclosed housing properties), has been communication via open face-to-face discussions, the Internet, signs and marches.

The success of this movement has been remarkable. Until its beginning in September 2011, the focus of most political discussions in the U.S. was on reducing government expenditures and the size of government and on fiscal austerity generally, with only a few, lonely voices calling for higher taxes on the rich and corporations. But even these modest calls attracted little support from Democrats and were rarely discussed in the media. Now that has changed dramatically as much of the nation is focusing on the concerns articulated by the Occupy movement. The change in the tone and content of political dialogue in the U.S. has been astonishing. One example was the sudden plethora of media articles, often in depth, about the growing inequality in income and wealth and about the influence of the rich and powerful on the political process. Even within the Republican party there has been an impact. Many doubt that Gingrich would have attacked Romney so strongly about his wealth (which is more than that of the last 10 Presidents *combined*) had it not been for the Occupy movement. As a leader of the Communication Workers of America union, Robert Master, said: "In three months, this movement succeeded in shifting political discourse more than labor had been able to accomplish with years of lobbying and electoral campaigns." (New York Times, Feb 12, 2012)

At the same time, many of the encampments that initially were often supported by their local city governments, soon became unacceptable to those same agencies. While all the cities said that they supported the "right to demonstrate," they were unwilling to allow "camping," that is, sleeping and eating in tents over an extended period. Some acknowledged that the tents were a form of symbolic speech, others refused to accept that premise. (In part, each encampment became a focal point for the local homeless to stay at, which was welcomed by the Occupy people, but resisted by city officials, who claimed deteriorating health and safety conditions.) But the Occupy movements in virtually all of these cities have stayed intact in various forms and continue to mount regular demonstrations, putting down roots in city after city, sometimes working out of donated office space and meeting in churches and other public spaces. In early February, Occupy activists, mainly from New York, undertook a five-week bus tour to forge personal links, exchange ideas and hold training sessions with like-minded activists.

The Future of the Occupy Movement

What impact the Occupy movement will ultimately have on the American public, on the various agencies of government, and on the Congressional and Presidential election campaigns now underway remains to be seen. But it is quite clear that this movement seems determined to endure, and most observers expect it to expand anew in the spring and summer of 2012. The New York Times recently (2/12/12) reported that "Far from dissipating, groups around the country say they are preparing for a new phase of larger marches and strikes this spring that they hope will rebuild momentum and cast an even brighter glare on inequality and corporate greed." Building on a proposal that originated in Portland, Oregon, groups in 34 cities have reportedly agreed to "a day of nonviolent direct action on Feb 29th against corporations working against the public interest." Plans are currently underway for large demonstrations across the nation on May 1st . This includes a possible call for something in the nature of a general strike where the 99% show their power by withholding their labor for a day. However, so far, the labor movement, which would be crucial to the success of such a strike, seems cool to the suggestions. Nevertheless, as the labor leader quoted above said: "We have different roles – as labor we are much more embedded in mainstream politics. But we understand that without the pressure of more radical direct-action tactics, the debate in this country won't change substantially."

The Occupy Movement remains alive and well, and we shall all simply have to wait to see what its future will be.

This piece was also published in the Dutch journal Streven: A Journal of Political Economy.

How to Run a Stimulus Program: Include Loans (Issue #20)

By Bob Gerecke

The government loaned money to General Motors (and others) because they were too big to fail. The government (we the citizens) made money on the deal. Why not expand the loan program during a recession/depression to businesses and citizens whose individual failure would not wreck the economy but whose collective failures would?

Preventing a federal budget deficit of more than 3% in any year, as some have suggested (including Warren Buffett, possibly in jest), will be catastrophic when we again have a depression or severe recession.

Because tax revenues decline under those circumstances, it will force the national government to cut its spending just when state and local governments, businesses, families and nonprofits are doing the same. This will make the downturn worse, which in turn will further reduce government tax collections, forcing a further cutback and further increasing the downturn. It will be a vicious cycle creating a downward economic spiral. The government can't raise taxes to reduce the deficit, either, without increasing the downturn. In addition, during a time of major war, like WW II, which may happen again some day, the government will be inhibited from fully funding our military.

Some have suggested averaging annual surpluses and deficits to balance out over a 7 or 10 year period, i.e., a complete economic cycle. However, the economic cycle isn't always of the same length, so eventually the country will find itself needing stimulus when it can't be offered without exceeding the balance.

An even better alternative is for the government to have two flexible strategies: one for businesses, one for individuals and families. The government should loan stimulus funds to businesses which were viable before the downturn. The government did this when bailing out the mega-banks, AIG and auto manufacturers. The government should expand this tactic beyond the "too big to fail" companies, because the economy itself can't be allowed to fail. The loans will be paid off as the economy improves. Loans won't add to the national debt, because the government's loan assets will balance the debits it incurs by selling Treasury bonds.

The loans can be made by the Federal Reserve itself. The Fed's actions are never exactly at the best time and in the best amount, but the Fed has learned and improved, which cannot be said of the Congress. The Fed's decisions are flexible in response to economic data, because the Board members are not hobbled by political ideology or by the need to satisfy a political base. A study made a few years ago revealed that the Fed staff's forecasts of future economic conditions have been more accurate than those of any other major financial institution. The Fed will do as good a job as any merely human institution can do to manage the timing and amount of stimulus.

How will it work? The Fed can charge businesses the same variable interest rate it charges banks: starting very low when stimulus is most needed, rising as the economy recovers. The interest and principal payments can be structured as a percent of taxable income and collected via the IRS, thereby collecting them efficiently and only as the debtor has the ability to pay. A struggling business can look at its own financial circumstances and decide whether or not to borrow; those with liquid assets might not, at least until they begin to run out of cash. The amount of the loan can be based on a reasonable estimate of the business' future earnings after economic recovery. The borrower can pay off the loan quickly or all at once if able to do so.

To aid unemployed individuals and families, the government should adopt a four-pronged approach:

1. The Fed should offer loans to them on the same basis as the loans proposed above for businesses. This will be necessary if Congress and the President fail to establish the laws and appropriations for the other three prongs below, and some persons may choose this option even if the others are available.

The ability to offer loans to either or both businesses and consumers will enable the Fed to support the supply side and/or demand side of the economy, as needed. At present, it doesn't have the ability to target one side or the other, but can only raise or lower interest rates on everyone, which is a crude tool when demand must be increased to absorb supply or vice-versa.

2. The government should ramp up public employment and contracting for socially and economically beneficial work such as repair and construction of infrastructure, installation of broadband and renewable energy, environmental restoration, medical and other scientific research, drug rehabilitation, crime prevention, and data gathering for economic, social and medical planning.

There is always much work left undone, and the best time to do it is when many people of many talents as well as work space and supplies are most available, without causing inflation by competing with the private sector for resources. The needs can be identified and plans to meet them can be drawn up in advance, so the work can begin quickly.

The New Deal of the 1930's bequeathed us cleared swamps, hydroelectric power, rural electrification, post offices, libraries, highways, levees, improved agricultural methods and many other resources which still benefit us. Its model should be the norm, not the exception.

3. High unemployment is the perfect time for people to increase their skills by attending night school, trade school or university; government stipends to the students and the schools should be available for that. The country's people will emerge more employable and productive. It will also provide teaching employment for possessors of skills who are temporarily unemployed.

The temporary government jobs and student stipends should pay less than the same people will earn in the private sector, so they will take other jobs as soon as possible, thereby reducing the public payroll as the economy recovers.

4. The government should incentivize and enable homeowners to remain in their homes even if they are under water, i.e., if their mortgage debt exceeds the temporarily reduced value of their homes. Measures to accomplish this include principal reduction, interest rate reduction and payment holidays. Recalcitrant banks can be brought on board by the threat of eminent domain and by legislation requiring that defaulting homeowners by given the right to meet the highest bid for their home or to lease their home at market rate.

Despite the short-term costs of these proposals, the government should come out ahead over the long term, as follows:

The loan programs will increase the Fed's overhead from the cost of administering the loans. This cost will lower the Fed's payments of its income, after expenses, to the U.S. Treasury, until the loan repayments exceed the costs. In addition, there will be some defaults. However, the stimulus provided by business loans, public employment and contracting, education stipends and mortgage cost reductions will support consumer spending, business revenues and hiring, thereby minimizing defaults by borrowers. Overall, the government probably will not take a loss on the loans, but will eventually make a profit instead, because the stimulus should increase government revenues enough, and reduce demands on the social safety net enough, to more than compensate for the defaults and for the increase in Fed overhead.

The temporary increase in government employment and education stipends will directly cost substantial sums of money and will increase the national debt in the short term. However, the resulting benefits will increase economic activity, productivity, Gross Domestic Product and government tax revenues for the long haul, while the temporary expenditures will automatically decrease as the economy recovers, thereby enabling the government to reduce its debt over time.

In addition, families and businesses will be saved

from bankruptcy, which is the point of it all anyway. Government isn't a business which exists to improve its own financial statement; it exists to benefit the public, and it will have fulfilled its purpose if it does so.

Why not simply have the government guarantee loans made by private banks when economic stimulus is needed? Two reasons:
1) We have learned the hard way that we can't trust the banks to estimate future ability to pay when they make a loan, as long as the risk of loss because of default isn't theirs.
2) In order to maximize profit, banks will add to loan costs (as they have done to government-guaranteed mortgages and student loans) either by charging a higher interest rate, or by adding fees, or both, which will reduce the stimulus effect of the loans on the rest of the economy.

If the government guarantees most but not all of each loan, banks will be too restrictive in extending credit, as we have seen during the recent recession and recovery, because they fear some losses from defaults, yet they will not receive the compensating tax increases from the economic rebound. If they are given the compensating tax increases, their loans will then be guaranteed in full; as argued above, this is dangerous.

Furthermore, if the government has to judge which bank loan to guarantee in full and which only in part, if at all, it will require government to duplicate the private underwriting, a waste of money and effort.

Therefore, the most efficient method will be for the government not to guarantee bank loans but to underwrite and make loans itself. During a recession or depression, there will be no shortage of experienced loan underwriters to hire and of office space to house them.

Why not have the government subsidize private businesses to hire people? If a business uses the employees to do its usual work, it will be over-staffed in relation to customer demand, and no beneficial work will result. If the business uses the employees to do the government work described above, however, this will make sense when the business has expertise in the work which government managers and staff lack. That's why contracting as well as public employment is mentioned in the above proposal. Contracting should be used only when necessary, though, since it will increase government costs: the businesses will charge the government a profit margin which, unlike a loan, the government will not recover later.

These are not new ideas. Only the proposal for direct lending to businesses and consumers is a recent entry to the discussion. It adapts proposals by Stephen Zarlenga and Ellen Brown (his that the government issue money instead of borrowing it, and hers that there be a public bank) to the existing Federal Reserve structure, and it follows a Bush-Obama precedent.

Basically we know what can be done to counter a downturn; the only thing lacking is the cooperation of conservative fanatics in Congress, who would rather see our economy deteriorate and people suffer than see a Democratic administration accomplish anything which the public will appreciate.

Beyond Regulation v Deregulation (Issue #9)
By Ivan Light

We American progressives aim to overcome the conservative drive to leave businesses free to do as they will. Public good cannot be served that way. But we also need to propose mechanisms to sort out desirable from undesirable regulations. Perhaps the conservative rant against regulations as such could be softened if there were some administrative court for businesses to plead their case against specific regulations.

I recently spent a half hour with a fellow from Philadelphia who owns a big commercial bakery there. His bakery makes and distributes bread and cakes to supermarkets in the region. This business owner spent that half hour telling me the problems his business faces with government regulation. He was quite indignant, and thought that government regulations (county, state, and federal) were trying to compel him to sell for three dollars what it costs him four to produce. As a result, he was desperately considering what options he might have to shift production to the American South or even offshore. The undesirable result of government regulation was job loss in his opinion. Did I, a known liberal, really want that, he wondered?

As the discussion progressed, it became clear that to this business owner the political issue at stake was regulation vs. deregulation. That is, in his opinion, the government regulates his business now, the cost of regulation is unacceptably high, and the result has been the creation of financial incentives to relocate his business to a low-regulation environment someplace else. Well, what's his solution? In his opinion, the solution is total deregulation of his industry, wholesale bakeries. The government should stop regulating his industry, said he, and just let him make bread and cake in Philadelphia as he best devises, subject only to the competition of other bakeries. This opinion echoes Ronald Reagan, who famously said "Government is not the solution; government is the problem."

Of course, I could not explain away nor condone the various examples of maladroit government policy that bedevil the bakery industry in Philadelphia. What do I know about the wholesale bakery industry in Philadelphia? I had to agree with him that the examples of maladroit regulations that he offered sounded unwise and counterproductive, and should be abolished. In fact, I *do agree* with him about that. We *should* abolish regulations that unreasonably and counterproductively hamstring business, and the sooner the better! But that is not the same as agreeing that all economic regulation of industry is undesirable and should be abolished, which was his program. Wholesale abolition was his nostrum, and, as is well known, it's also the nostrum peddled by conservatives.

Wrong issue! The issue is not pro-regulation vs. deregulation. The issue is not deregulation at all. Recall that lack of regulation led to the financial crisis of 2008; lack of regulation led to the BP oil spill in the Gulf of Mexico; lack of regulation gave us air and water pollution and global warming; lack of regulation brings spoiled meat and poisonous vegetables to supermarket shelves; lack of regulation brings unsafe drugs to pharmacy shelves. The USA cannot just abolish government regulation of business.

The real issue is how to regulate most effectively. Effective regulation eliminates or minimizes undesirable restraints on business while retaining the desirable restraints. Effective regulation involves sifting and sorting what is helpful and what is not. Americans do indeed want to prevent companies from dumping their toxic waste into our water supply, the cheapest disposal solution for them, and government regulation of business is how we prevent them from poisoning us. Is there an alternative method?

On the other hand, we do not want to impose useless or excessive regulation on any business. Therefore, America's problem is not regulation vs. deregulation as it's commonly introduced by the media, by the right, and by the business owner from Philadelphia. The problem is how to improve regulation.

What can be done to focus public attention around the terminally boring issue of how best to regulate business? First, we need to explain again and again why this boring issue is important so that people can understand why they should care. That's what I am doing right here. Hey, you, wake up! People should care about government regulation because their jobs, their health, and their children's future are at stake. Second, we need to make clear that American progressives stand for *effective but minimal regulation of business*. That is, we progressives advocate the absolute minimum of government regulation that is necessary to protect the public safety and health. But we absolutely insist on protecting the public against what economists call "negative externalities" e.g. the production of harmful by-products for the public as a result of commercial business. They frack and as a result we drink toxic water. The public gets polluted water, and the oil companies get profits. Does this sound right to you?

How can we accomplish effective regulation? First, we can make more use of sunset provisions. All government regulations of business should expire automatically every three or four years unless renewed. A regulations commission should sit continuously, its function to examine expiring regulations, to weigh their desirability, and, if found undesirable, to allow them automatically to expire while recommending for renewal those regulations found to be in the public interest. If a sunset commission existed, the owner of the Philadelphia bakery would have an opportunity to explain why burdensome regulations should be abolished; and, by golly, he might be right. Second, commissioners should be protected against cooptation from the industries they purport to regulate by whatever devices we can set in place, including high salaries on the one hand, and imprisonment for corruption on the other.

These are initial thoughts indeed, and they should and can be improved in Congress, but even these simple reflections shift the debate from "regulation vs. deregulation" to "how best to regulate." This is the debate we Americans need to have.

Regulation, Incomes and Prosperity (Issue #15)

By Ivan Light

Increased regulations are the price business pays for increased economic growth – conservatives don't get it!

In a previous piece on the TAIPD website (Issue #9, April 2012), I explained that conservative complaints about regulation have some validity. Government regulation of business can be and sometimes is excessive, ineffective, and counter-productive. It's always a pain-in-the-neck for business that regulation tends to raise the price of goods and reduce employment in affected industries.

That acknowledged, as earlier explained, government regulation of business is nonetheless a necessary evil because the alternative of non-regulation is worse. In the same sense, brakes detract from a car's performance, but they are nonetheless essential.

Non-regulation's consequences include reckless pollution of air, water, and soil; diseased meat sold in supermarkets; dangerous & gas-guzzling automobiles; incompetent medical doctors; lying advertisements for bogus products; cigarettes sold to minors, and the list goes on. Add your favorites.

Insisting on regulation that protects the public welfare, liberals want to minimize (not eliminate) essential regulation of business, and seek as well to produce regulations that provide the beneficial consequences desired. Regulations that do not accomplish these goals should be promptly scrapped. I suggested previously the use of sunset commissions that review all government regulations every four or five years, and mark some for discontinuation and others for change.

There is another important point to make about government regulation of business. Context matters. A desirable public policy would call for greater equality of incomes than currently prevails. One method of achieving that is heavy taxation of very high incomes. Another method is light taxation of low incomes. The upshot of both in tandem is greater income equality than unfettered capitalism provides.

The advantages of enhanced equality of income are many, both social and economic, but I mention here only the systematic correction of capitalism's inherent and invariant tendency to tilt the distribution of income toward the wealthy with calamitous results for employment. Left to themselves, market economies too generously reward the very affluent, and starve the ninety-nine percent. As John Maynard Keyes long ago pointed out, working people spend every dime they get; and the rich save their millions.

As a result, in a crisis of under-consumption, such as we now face, the 99 percent lack the financial wherewithal to buy the output of the economy. Goods are unsold. For example, many unemployed people live now under overcrowded conditions, homeless, or in dilapidated shelters, yet new homes stand empty. Unfortunately, the under housed cannot buy the empty homes so they remain empty, and the unemployed suffer overcrowding.

When working people lack money, because too much money belongs to the wealthy, the result is mass unemployment. To offset their low incomes, the American people overused credit for two decades, borrowing the wherewithal to buy what their paychecks were too meager to purchase, especially houses; but that credit bubble burst in 2008. Now we starkly confront the fact that the affluent one percent with money will not spend it, and the ninety-nine percent lack sufficient money to purchase essentials.

What does the unequal division of incomes have to do with government regulation of business? Plenty. Consider this. Liberal administrations introduce an economic policy favoring enhanced government regulation of business *plus a regime* of increased equalization of incomes. The two policies come together, not separately. The enhanced income equality creates buyer demand in the marketplace, which makes it easier for business to sell its products. Business is able to sell because customers have the money to buy. Therefore, when a liberal, progressive, administration reduces inequality of income, they create consumer demand that advantages business. True, they *also impose* regulations that restrict business. These restrictions limit the range of products that can be brought to market, and tend to raise their price. But, the point is that business gets compensation for that added hurdle of regulation: increased consumer demand.

Now consider the conservative option. Under conservative administrations the opposite policies are put into place: enhanced inequality of income accompanies reduced regulation of business. So the conservative allows business immense latitude of action, ignoring the public interest, but reduces the ability of business to find buyers for its products. In an extreme case, business can bring whatever junk it likes to market (spoiled meat, dangerous or useless pharmaceuticals, unsafe & gas-guzzling vehicles, collapsing bridges, etc.) and recklessly despoil the environment, injuring the public's health, but the marketplace still contains insufficient buyers with money in their patched and worn blue jeans. Do you want to buy horsemeat because it's cheap and, lacking money, you have no other option? Or would you prefer to afford sirloin? Worse, buying the crummy stuff does not produce full employment because the public lacks the money to pay for it.

This is the awful choice the right offers America. Such an outcome injures business, workers, and consumers alike. Under such policies, Americans must live in polluted squalor, and unemployment continues to stalk the land. This is a dreadful outcome, and it explains why economic growth under liberal administrations in the last fifty years has been more than twice as rapid as economic growth under conservative administrations during the same period.

Enhanced economic growth is the compensation business receives for enhanced regulation.

Is Our Regulatory System Working? (Issue #19)

By John Grula

The continuing story of how a private utility giant in California gets away with illegal activity, including destruction of evidence thanks to a cozy relationship with the state agency supposedly regulating it. Publically owned companies are the answer.

On Jan. 14, the California Public Utilities Commission (CPUC) released a long-delayed final report on the performance of investor-owned Southern California Edison (SCE) during the severe windstorm that struck Pasadena and surrounding communities on the night of Nov. 30/Dec. 1, 2011. During the storm, more than 440,000 SCE customers (households and businesses) lost power that, in some cases, was not restored for more than a week. The black-out rate in the San Gabriel Valley areas served by SCE approached 100 percent.

SCE's windstorm performance was so bad that the CPUC launched an investigation shortly after the storm ended. In stark contrast, the CPUC did not investigate community-owned Pasadena Water and Power, which came out of the storm smelling like a rose (so to speak). Even though Pasadena was ground zero for the most destructive wind gusts during the storm, only about 10 percent of its customers lost power, and nearly all of those who did had it restored within a few days.

Almost exactly one year ago, the CPUC issued a scathing preliminary report that found, among other things, that at least 20 of the more than 200 SCE power poles that were blown down or badly damaged during the storm were overloaded with cables and equipment. This means pole overloading was a primary cause of why so many SCE poles went down or were damaged during the storm. It is also a violation of state law subject to potential penalties.

The final CPUC report issued Jan. 14 was equally critical of SCE and also admonished the utility for destroying crucial evidence. In a Jan. 15 story in the Pasadena Star-News, Temple City Councilman Tom Chavez was quoted saying, "I am especially disappointed in the lack of preservation of evidence by SCE, which not only hindered the investigation, but could have helped in determining how to avoid future accidents." In a Jan. 16 editorial, the newspaper stated that "so much evidence was in fact destroyed that investigators were only able to fully reconstruct five power poles out of many dozens they had wanted to see."

So SCE was, at the very least, guilty of pole overloading and destruction of evidence. Both are illegal, right? But other than reporting these violations of the law, what did the CPUC do? Instead of penalizing Edison, it made six "recommendations" to SCE that included updating its emergency procedures, following a training schedule and testing its emergency response plan with a full-scale exercise on an annual basis. But these are all after-the-fact actions that have nothing to do with the illegal acts of pole overloading and the destruction of evidence. Where's the justice in this? People and businesses suffered mightily because of SCE's failures, but so far the utility has been given a free pass. According to a Jan. 20 newspaper report, CPUC officials have said they "will consider formal enforcement action and possible monetary penalties should SCE not comply satisfactorily with the problems identified in its report." Don't hold your breath.

The final CPUC report released on Jan. 14 was supposed to have been made public in early August (according to CPUC spokesperson Terrie Prosper in April). Why the long delay? Chavez blames the destruction of evidence for hindering the investigation. His point is well taken. But is it also possible the CPUC dragged its feet because it wanted more time for the public outrage over SCE's lousy performance to subside, thereby decreasing the possibility that people would notice the CPUC did not throw the book at SCE?

This raises a further question: Why did the CPUC treat SCE with kid gloves? It is pertinent to note that Michael R. Peevey, who has been the president of the CPUC for the last 10 years, is a former president of Edison International and SCE and served as a senior executive there from 1984 to 1995. This revolving door situation casts grave doubt on Mr. Peevey's ability to adjudicate issues with SCE without any bias or conflict of interest. Mr. Peevey is also compromised by the fact that SCE, its affiliates and employees have been major contributors to the campaign coffers of Peevey's wife, Democratic state Sen. Carol Liu of La Cañada Flintridge.

Finally, Mr. Peevey's reluctance to penalize SCE for breaking the law may also have something to do with his acute awareness of the current problems

Edison is having with its San Onofre nuclear power station on the San Diego County coast. Equipment failures at this plant may also be the result of SCE malfeasance. Repair costs and possible monetary penalties could approach $1 billion.

Nevertheless, until SCE is punished for breaking the law, we will continue to have more power outage disasters like the one San Gabriel Valley residents were forced to endure in December 2011.

This article was originally published in the Pasadena Weekly on Feb 13, 2013.

The Ant and the Grasshopper: A Response from the Left (Various Issues 2011-2013)

by Merrill Ring

If Aesop the slave did write the Ant and the Grasshopper fable, he would today be rightly labeled a conservative, a darling of the right-wing. For there is no doubt that the tale favors the Ant, who labors hard all summer, laying in food for the winter, while the Grasshopper enjoys himself; but come the winter the Grasshopper then needs the good will of the Ant who refuses to give it.

For centuries now, the fable has been used by conservatives (by whatever name they called themselves) to justify their ways and attitudes. And those on the other side of the fence have made reply.

But of course one cannot find any response by the conservatives to the criticism of their Ant worship.

We find today an up-to-date version of the fable made familiar in right-wing circles by one of their shrews, Michelle Malkin. And so we critics of those views need to produce yet another criticism of the fable, thinking to once again negate Ant worship, though without hope that it will soon vanish.

The fable creates a world in which there are only two beings: the Ant and the Grasshopper. It opens: *"Once there lived an ant and a grasshopper in a grassy meadow."*

We progressives (or social democrats or modern liberals) must criticize those very opening words of the fable. For its aim is precisely to eliminate the social background of human life and to make its moral point as if ants and grasshoppers, and so too human beings, are fully formed atoms without regard to their fellow creatures and their institutions.

The ant in the fable does not live in an anthill and so has no culture to form it and no fellows to support it. It is a self-made ant. And equally the grasshopper is to be taken to be cultureless, to be free of any influences on its way of life not deriving from its own natural being.

That is, whatever good or bad accrues to them

will be solely and totally a matter of their own doing. The Ant is that paragon of the right, the self-made man who owes nothing to anybody else or to the social world (and even the natural world) into which it is born and develops. The Self-made Ant/Human Being is a product solely of his own self and especially his own effort. The Grasshopper, on the other hand, is a lazy lay-about, who could have been providing for his own well-being but instead prefers to do nothing but enjoy himself: no one else is around to share his responsibility for his life and his problems. He is a self-made failure.

One of the basic tenets of modern liberalism or social democracy (or whatever the outlook is called) is that that picture of human atoms whose characteristics are not at all shaped by others or by the social world in which they find themselves is totally false. It is disagreement about that picture that creates a fundamental division between conservatives and social democrats.

It is tempting to turn to the important topic of just why modern liberals reject the individualistic assumptions of conservative social theory, to remind ourselves of why it is important to see people as social beings. (The topic today goes under the heading of *the social conditions for freedom* in the political philosophy, political theory literature.) But that will have to wait for later. Ants and Grasshoppers are the topic here.

In any grassy meadow, there is not a solitary ant and a solitary grasshopper. In fact, since ants are highly social and cooperative creatures, even more organized than we liberals can accept as a model for human life, Aesop's fable must be restructured from the start. Something like: "In a grassy meadow was an ant colony. In the morning, the scouts went out to determine where the ants should spend the day. A straw boss assigned crews to various parts of the meadow and each unit went off to perform its day's work, bringing food back to the communal larder in the colony."

In the fable, however, Ant is alone in the grassy meadow (ignoring for now the Grasshopper), having no friends or family, life, no institutional framework, no history. What kind of life does she (or he) have? Work.

All day long the ant would work hard, collecting grains of wheat from the farmer's field far away. She would hurry to the field every morning, as soon as it was light enough to see by, and toil back with a heavy grain of wheat balanced on her head. She would put the grain of wheat carefully away in her larder, and then hurry back to the field for another one. All day long she would work, without stop or rest, scurrying back and forth from the field, collecting the grains of wheat and storing them carefully in her larder."

It is impossible to understand the conservative hatred (yes hatred) for welfare, for transfer payments to the unemployed, especially to those with long term unemployment but even to those who have a shorter spell out of work, without understanding the conservative attitude toward work. And that attitude is best expressed in the tale of Ant. So do not take the above passage, which is the picture of the Ant's labors, lightly.

The conservative's aim in the fable is to express first that the Ant is virtuous and in that excellence owes nothing to anyone else (except perhaps implicitly to the farmer, who is not a conservative on this matter since he does not insist that every grain of wheat is rightfully his because he has produced it). Moreover, the Ant is to be taken as the model of the good human life. What does the Ant do? Work. Work is what it is to be human. Further there is a conception of what work is that is embodied in the Ant's story, especially in the paragraph above, a conception that is pure conservative doctrine. Work, what life is all about on this view, is incessant, repetitive and uninteresting in itself: in a word, work is grim drudgery. And as work is the core of life, life is ....

The dwarves' song ' Just whistle while you work' is complete anathema to the conservatives. It is impossible, they hold, to be cheerful in work and life – or if you are, as are the dwarves, that is 'false consciousness', an attempt to hide from oneself the reality of what it is like to live and work.

But is work really incessant, repetitive and uninteresting?

That is an accurate description of what it was,

174

and is, like to work on an orthodox assembly line, say in a Henry Ford factory. The autos being assembled come past you on the line and you have one and only one task: to see that nut N is put on bolt B as each auto moves on down the line as they do inexorably. And you have to rise early in the morn, at least six days a week, and put in a ten hour day doing nothing but that, no breaks except a brief lunch stop. That is how you spend your life for, say, 40 years.

There are three things that must be said in reply to the conservative story: much work is not like being on an old fashioned line, is not like the Ant's labors; secondly, that contrary to the conservative view, it is possible to make things better, to improve the nature of work and thus our lives, to make our labors unlike the Ant's; third it is possible to diminish the extent of work so we do not live like the Ant but create a fuller and richer human life.

Let me point out one further thing about the fable. Notice that the translation above refers to the Ant as "she". In the new conservative Michelle Malkin' version the Ant is 'he'. Now I have no idea what, in the original Greek, the pronoun is – and I'm not going to find out. What is interesting is that the conservatives vacillate in their ways of telling the story, in their account of the gender of the Ant. That is one sign that they are talking of work, any work, all work, women's work, man's work: whoever you are, whatever you do, work is never done, repetitious and not, in itself, of any interest to anyone.

Why is the Ant in Aesop's fable a heroine or hero of conservatives?

There are several reasons. One I have already pointed out is that the Ant is a solitary, living in no social order and having no help and companionship. The conservative picture embodied in the Ant is that we humans should be, and heroic humans actually are, complete individuals, shaped only by oneself and relying upon no one else to make one's way through life.

But there is a second reason, something that we progressives tend to lose sight of. The conservative has, to its mind, a very important conception of work and of its place in human lives: the Ant exemplifies that conception. We progressives tend to overlook such that fact: for we do not have a corresponding and competing conception. Rather, it is the criticism of that conception that is important to our outlook.

Recall how Ant spends her/his time, at least during the productive summer months. "*All day long the ant would work hard, collecting grains of wheat from the farmer's field far away. She would hurry to the field every morning, as soon as it was light enough to see by, and toil back with a heavy grain of wheat balanced on her head. She would put the grain of wheat carefully away in her larder, and then hurry back to the field for another one. All day long she would work, without stop or rest, scurrying back and forth from the field, collecting the grains of wheat and storing them carefully in her larder.*"

I suspect that the Biblical story of Adam and Eve remains behind how conservatives see our relation to work. Since the original pair, representatives of humanity, were booted from Paradise, they, we, are condemned to a life of hard toil. "Cursed shall be the ground because of you; in sorrow you shall eat of it all the days of your life. And thorns and thistles it shall bring forth for you, and you shall eat the plant of the field. By the sweat of your face you shall eat bread until you return to the ground." (Genesis, 3:17-19)

Work, nasty in nature as the conservatives see it, is a central feature of human lives.

Of course, there are always some people who for various reasons (the pre-lapsarian Adam and Eve, the village idiot as well as the Duke, the kept woman, those with large inherited wealth, and the devil of the conservatives, the layabout (see the Grasshopper in the fable)) do not work. However, overwhelmingly people (including the traditional housewife doing her unremunerated tasks) do and must work. So first of all the Ant in the fable is iconic for conservatives as it expresses that understanding of human life.

That, though, is not anything liberal, progressive, even radical opponents of conservativism deny.

What the conservative wildly overdoes, and what does merit scorn, is the comparison of very many human lives to the Ant. The model for the Ant's labors is the slave (which is what author of the fable was) or the assembly line worker, a very limited selection of the working lives of humans. Note: conservatives have not been found applauding the heroism of the assembly line worker or the sweatshop worker, though they do celebrate that kind of life when it comes to the Ant. Is that not inconsistency?

Progressives must recognize this amount of truth in the conservative picture: there is much in most people's work that is drudgery, boring and destructive of the best in us. However, no matter how difficult work is generally, some employments are worse than others: and the fable chooses the most plodding of all as showing the real nature of work and of what it is to be human.

Does Michelle Malkin and company really think that they themselves are like the Ant as they go about earning their daily bread? How many people do they know whose actual working lives are comparable to the Ant? I wager: None. Yet they seemingly love Ant and generalize wildly from its life.

We should all recall that the left has (at least) two very excellent pieces of writing which do talk about the working lives of ordinary people: Studs Terkel's magnificent *Working* and Barbara Ehrenreich's *Nickled and Dimed*. We need to re-read those now.

The human analogs to the ant – where we ignore its postulated absolute solitude – are likely to form unions, have formed unions, where workers can act to overcome the dreariness and worse of their working conditions. Do the conservatives applaud these attempts to rid working people of drudgery and worse?

Of course not – such joint self-help organizations are anathema to the conservative. For the true hero is Ant who does not indulge in joining with others to help each other.

And that brings us to the second item in the conservative conception of work: the idea that work is always to be like the Ant's labors (remember the curse placed on Adam and Eve) and we must not try to make it better.

Compare how the conservative thinks of the situation of the Ant in Aesop's fable with what a progressive, a modern liberal, would say.

To the conservative, Ant is a hero for grindingly going on, day after day, with her/his labor. Work, conceived of as misery, is part of the very constitution of the universe and so it is something about which nothing can be done.

To the progressive such obnoxious styles of work as that of the assembly line, the sweatshop, the slave, the salary-man, child-labor and so on – the models for the conservative picture of work - are, in their various ways, capable of improvement, even elimination. It is assumed that we, both the progressive and the downtrodden workers, must rise up against that kind of labor, must join together to make their work and their lives better.

The conservative prefers hero-worship – the Heroic Ant - to joining together to eliminate or change obnoxious types of labor. (The Ant of course has no fellows to band together with – and not even an employer to rise up against.) Again, while it is not part of conservative practice to actually praise workers who have lives like that of Ant, they ought to be doing that as a consequence of their outlook. The failure to love those who labor shows that it is the literary expression of the view that they love, not actual people who earn their daily bread in such ways.

The number of ways in which working life has improved for human analogs of the Ant is too vast to catalog here (even if I could.) Let me insert something from Charles Bayer.

Whether you are a fan of unions or you are not, all of us are far better off today because of the hard-fought victories they have won. Do you covet your right to work-free weekends? Then you must give organized labor the credit. American business did not agree to a forty-hour week out of a generous spirit. This right was the product of hard-fought organized power.

The lives of Americans (and Europeans and no doubt others too) are much better today because we progressives have supported and worked for changes in the nature of work. We have achieved changes that the conservative conception of the place of work in the world assumes to be not possible.

The conservative conception of work embodied in the person (?) of Ant is flawed in at least three ways: it rests upon a picture of the nature of work (the model is the slave, the house maid or the assembly line worker) that is too narrow and thus does not accurately portray the variety of kinds of work that human beings engage in; it also represents work as unchangeable drudgery and refuses to see the vast improvements made in many people's work life over the past couple of hundred years and the possibilities for even more.

The third failure is this: the Ant has no other life than work. In this conservative picture, work is life, there is nothing worth remarking on outside it. The Ant has no social life, no television even, nothing to do after the daily fetching and carrying but wait for the next day with maybe a little laundry and house-cleaning tossed in.

The progressive vision includes the idea that there are other things in life than work that are humanly valuable and which need to be fostered both individually and socially. The liberal vision even includes the possibility that the work might someday be made not just less onerous (which has been happening now for a couple of centuries) but become not even the central feature of human life, to be replaced in importance by those other activities ignored or slighted by the conservative mind. It was one of the glories of the 1960's that that possibility was actively discussed. It is a theme that needs to be taken up again by progressives.

There are those who say 'Wait until we have returned to a settled economic condition before we start considering lives without work.' There is something to that: however, all those many people who presently are long-term unemployed, maybe now permanently so, might be brought to see that there is life not just after but without work (if you can get enough to eat.)

This completes the critical analysis of the Ant in the fable – a question remains. Do contemporary conservatives, including those who are resurrecting Aesop's fable, really believe the conception of work found in the story? Or is just their hatred of the Grasshopper that inclines them to mouth a more traditional conservative idea of the nature and place of work in human life? I have my suspicions that it is really the latter, that the so-called present conservatives are not really traditional conservatives at all except when it suits them.

So far, in looking into the fable of the Ant and the Grasshopper, I've been examining that hero of conservatives, the Ant. What appeals to conservatives in that character is his or her atomism – the solitary figure going on with life without any supporting social institutions or even other 'people'. And what is that life the Ant is leading? It is work: the Ant embodies a conservative conception of life as unrelenting toil, accepted without demur.

Those conservative notions have been and should be the object of progressive criticism: we are not social atoms, the Ant's style of work is not the model of all work and such work, even work itself, need not be accepted as a fact of human existence of such significance as the conservatives makes of it.

For the modern conservative, the conception of human life as work is not the main attraction of Aesop's fable. Instead, it is the character of the Grasshopper, so far not examined, that is the center of modern conservative attention. While it is likely that our future economic arrangements will make the notion of work again more central to conservative views, it is to their hatred of the Grasshopper and what he stands for that we must now turn.

Note: whereas the Ant, in the history of the fable, is sometimes thought of as male and sometimes as female, the Grasshopper seems, at least in current thought, to be male (though the expression 'welfare queens' does suggest that females can play the role as well.)

At the start it is important to recognize that in the fable the Grasshopper as well as the Ant is conceived of as completely alone. There are no social institutions at all in the meadow – and the Grasshopper is also not given any fellows. The idea of humans as fully formed solitaries – the Hobbesian picture – is crucial to the conservative love of the story, both in the character of the Ant and that of the Grasshopper as well. The individual in this view is completely responsible for whatever good or ill befalls them in the course of life.

Of course there is a huge hole in the story at this point: how does the Grasshopper support himself over the course of the summer? Perhaps he has caring friends or parents who, off-stage, bring him food daily. Those social institutions and other 'persons' missing in Aesop's story peek out from behind the structure here to remind us that the world is not as empty as the conservative myth has it.

The first thing to notice about the Grasshopper is

that when he is introduced into the story the initial contrast is between his attitude toward life and the Ant's.

All day long she would work, without stop or rest, scurrying back and forth from the field, collecting the grains of wheat and storing them carefully in her larder. The grasshopper would look at her and laugh. 'Why do you work so hard, dear ant?' he would say. 'Come, rest awhile, listen to my song. Summer is here, the days are long and bright. Why waste the sunshine in labour and toil?' The ant would ignore him, and head bent, would just hurry to the field a little faster.

The Grasshopper laughs – the Ant nowhere is presented as laughing. Of course, in the evening as she contemplates the increasing stock of wheat in her larder, she may have a small feeling of satisfaction – but then she remembers that tomorrow is another day and tomorrow's work must be prepared for tonight. There is no laughter in the Ant's world. I mentioned earlier that the song of Disney's dwarves in <u>Snow White</u>, 'Whistle while you work', is anathema to the conservative. Work is grim, life is without joy, with only small fleeting feelings of satisfaction when the current success of one's work is observed (though it may all fall apart tomorrow.) As Gary Wills noted in <u>*Nixon Agonistes*</u>, to the conservative character one must prove oneself anew every day: there is no resting on laurels, nothing more than a fleeting sense of a job well done.

The Grasshopper laughs both as an expression of joy at life, because of the beauty of the summer day and his engagement in the enjoyable activity of making music, but also laughs <u>at</u> the Ant, for her incessant labor when she too

184

could be enjoying the wonder around her. One may wish that the Grasshopper had not done that but, hey, we progressives are human too.

For the conservative, over and above those attitudes on the part of the Grasshopper, there are two important items in the story of the Grasshopper: what the Grasshopper is doing and what he is not doing.

The conservative criticism of the Grasshopper in Aesop's fable rests upon several different features of the Grasshopper's role. The Grasshopper's joy in life, his cheerfulness and laughter, runs completely contrary to how the conservative urges us to see life: there is no (legitimate) joy in Mudville or any other place of human habitation.

There are (at least) two other major sources of distaste for the Grasshopper, one obvious and one less so, one concerned with what he is not doing and one with what he is doing. Certainly the main theme is that the Grasshopper is not working, not gainfully employed, not planning for the future. However, consider what the Grasshopper *is* doing.

He is making music all the day, day after day.

He could have been represented as say napping constantly, or as (in a modern version) watching trash TV or reading comic books, or perhaps canoodling with an equally unemployed lady grasshopper (or two). But that is not how he spends his time. Rather he makes music.

The Grasshopper is a busker – though he doesn't even have his hat out for the passerby to drop in a coin or a grain of wheat in recognition of his providing enjoyment. At most he asks the Ant to pause, listen and enjoy.

Let me generalize and say that he is practicing Art, musical art: though he might have been writing poetry or fiction, or painting. And we must think that the fable is condemning him for indulging in an artistic pursuit when he should have been doing something that might be intrinsically worthless but that does earn one money for doing it.

Toni Morrison, who has won both the Nobel and Pulitzer prizes for her novels, has taken the time to help create a (picture) book about the Ant and the Grasshopper. (Toni & Slade Morrison, pictures by Pascal Lemaitre, *Who's Got Game: The Ant or the Grasshopper?*) It is an engaging retelling of the fable in a modern urban setting: and the question posed for thought by the (young) reader is 'Should one pursue one's artistic dream or must one choose work?' A line that should attract attention is the Grasshoppers's: "How can you say I've never worked a day? ART IS WORK – it just looks like play?" Well, says the conservative, it is not gainful work. (Unless of course it is – some do get paid for their artistic endeavors.)

While I was looking up the Morrisons' book on Amazon, I came across an Amazon review of it by someone who signs themselves 'Responsible Artist (At work making money so I can eat AND make art!)' The review is a perfect expression of the conservative picture of artistic production versus gainful employment. "It's ok to have an appreciation for the arts. What's NOT ok is the author's message to kids that it's ok to completely cast aside your responsibility to provide for yourself in the pursuit of your dream of being an artist. What would have been a better twist on this story is that in the end the ant was not only a responsible citizen but an artist as well. I don't recommend this version. Stick with the original Aesop's fable version. ART IS WORK but if nobody wants to buy it then you'd better be able to eat it."

We can be glad that the author does make the slight concession that art appreciation is ok. Whoopee! But the author mistakes the Morrison's message: it isn't that youthful readers are being encouraged to stick with their artistic dreams. Rather they are being asked to compare the two ways of life. Of course, in a world in which the views of Responsible Artist are the norm, the Morrisons try to give an equally strong voice to the other side. That is so far outside Responsible Artist's conservative vision of life that any encouragement to consider the pursuit of dreams as worthy of consideration can only be a recommendation to do so.

We more liberal people can try to think of all the various things that a young would-be-artist takes into consideration as they struggle with the problem of how to pursue their dream while needing to maintain themselves. Questions about the way they might live (would it suit them to be a hungry artist in a garret?), about how successful they might be as an artist, about whether economic conditions offer them a satisfying life outside art, about whether they can put together a life that involves working and saving for a while so that they can stop and return to what they want to do and so on. The conservative, embodied in Responsible Artist, isn't interested in those questions. Work first, then and only then think about whether you can find a way to do something artistic. Make money, live later!

Conservatives despise the Grasshopper because he is so cheerful and because he spends his (summer) days doing something low on the scale of human activity, namely making music, especially as he is not providing for himself, making money, by doing fiddling the day away.

But of course what he is most despised for is that he is NOT WORKING. He is able bodied, fully capable of remunerative work, but chooses not to.

He has not been laid off, is not the victim of economic hard times, is not between jobs: the conservative disapproves enough of people who find themselves in those circumstances. But the Grasshopper has made the choice not to work at a paying job in good times and that for the conservative is morally abominable.

It is even worse: he is enjoying himself in making music, i.e. enjoying himself in not working. And by making music in the meadow, along the path where the Ant trudges many times a day, day after day, he is tempting the virtuous Ant away from the path of righteousness. And in the story he goes so far as to try to get the Ant to stop that blind drive to acquire, to stop and enjoy the day:

"The grasshopper would look at her and laugh. 'Why do you work so hard, dear ant?' he would say. 'Come, rest awhile, listen to my song. Summer is here, the days are long and bright. Why waste the sunshine in labour and toil?' The ant would ignore him, and head bent, would just hurry to the field a little faster. This would make the grasshopper laugh even louder. 'What a silly little ant you are!' he would call after her. 'Come, come and dance with me! Forget about work! Enjoy the summer! Live a little!' And the grasshopper would hop away across the meadow, singing and dancing merrily."

Tempting the Ant to avoid work and thus away from the virtuous life makes the Grasshopper evil.

Now let's think a bit. The Ant is busy gathering the grains of wheat and storing them away for the season when the crop is finished. But surely during the summer she is consuming some of the wheat to keep herself going. Every night a little bowl of Cream of Wheat for dinner. However, the conservative version of the story doesn't even allow the Grasshopper that much: yet surely the question must come up: How does the Grasshopper survive the summer? Does he have parental support for his artistic endeavors? Do his friends supply him with the wherewithal to live during the good times? Has he worked, saved up and then quit in order to develop his musical abilities, living on what he saved? Did he inherit money? (The conservative

189

suspects that he is drawing welfare benefits of some sort, enabling him to avoid work.)

It is just here that my earlier analysis of the conservative picture of human life, that it consists and must consist of work, becomes relevant. Work is not enjoyable – that is why the Ant can be tempted even if heroically she overcomes the human temptation to not work, to avoid the necessary grind of acquiring one's daily bread, and thereby becomes even more morally virtuous. The Grasshopper, makes a choice to avoid the lot of humanity: and surely, for the conservative, a righteous universe will see to it that that choice is punished. And so we near the end of the tale.

There is one last piece of Aesop's fable to be considered, a conclusion that is dear to the conservative's heart.

Summer faded into autumn, and autumn turned into winter. The sun was hardly seen, and the days were short and grey, the nights long and dark. It became freezing cold, and snow began to fall. The grasshopper didn't feel like singing any more. He was cold and hungry. He had nowhere to shelter from the snow, and nothing to eat. The meadow and the farmer's field were covered in snow, and there was no food to be had. 'Oh what shall I do? Where shall I go?' wailed the grasshopper. Suddenly he remembered the ant. 'Ah - I shall go to the ant and ask her for food and shelter!' declared the grasshopper, perking up. So off he went to the ant's house and knocked at her door. 'Hello ant!' he cried cheerfully. 'Here I am, to sing for you, as I warm myself by your fire, while you get me some food from that larder of yours!'

The ant looked at the grasshopper and said, 'All summer long I worked hard while you made fun of me, and sang and danced. You should have thought of winter then! Find somewhere else to sing, grasshopper! There is no warmth or food for you here!' And the ant shut the door in the grasshopper's face.

Let us suppose that matters in the meadow are just as the conservative has claimed: Ant has worked the summer away without deviating from the daily routine of collecting and storing the (farmer's) wheat away in her larder, never giving in to the temptation offered by the grasshopper to join him in song and dance; Grasshopper was fully capable of working throughout the long summer days as did the ant and was not out of 'work' because of a seriously distressed economy but instead chose to make music, no doubt an enjoyable activity but one that produced no income. Fall and winter come and the grasshopper has no food saved for the hard times. Starving, he turns to the ant for assistance (in the fable, there is no one else in the meadow to turn to.)

As we see, Ant tells the truth (from her conservative point of view) about what has happened over the summer, slams the door in the grasshopper's face, leaving him, without question, to his deserts, to starvation.

There is no doubt that the conservative psyche

loves this conclusion: you will get no help from me for the outcome is exactly what you deserve, the result of your own choices about how to live, so accept the suffering.

What is the liberal to say? Let us make the case most difficult for our side. Suppose that the critique (produced earlier in this analysis) of the conservative position on all the issues that arise about the circumstances in the meadow is ignored and that consequently we let the conservative have the correct interpretation of those circumstances. The liberal still has to strongly object to the ant's behavior. For in the ant's behavior, and the conservatives' approval of it, is an unrelenting nastiness packaged as morality.

There is absolutely no mercy shown or to be shown. Recall that the Grasshopper has not harmed anyone else or the meadow, has not pillaged and plundered or savaged the local environment, but has simply not worked and not saved, has probably been irresponsible. He should be shut out to freeze to death for that? He deserves starvation for that?

It is not as if there is so little in the ant's larder that should she share it with the grasshopper, she will herself starve or even struggle to make it through the winter. She can well afford to help the grasshopper. But she doesn't – and the conservative will say she shouldn't. Conservative justice demands that.

What the conservative needs to be reminded of here is Portia's famous speech in <u>The</u> <u>Merchant</u> <u>of</u> <u>Venice:</u>

'"The quality of mercy is not srrain'd,
It droppeth as the gentle rain from heaven
Upon the place beneath: it is twice blest;
It blesseth him that gives and him that takes:
'Tis mightiest in the mightiest: it becomes
The throned monarch better than his crown;
His scepter shows the fore of temporal power,
The attribute to awe and majesty,
Wherein doth sit the dread and fear of kings;
But mercy is above this sceptered sway;
It is enthroned in the hearts of kings,
It is an attribute to God himself;
And earthly power doth then show likest God's
When mercy seasons justice. There, Jew,
Though just be thy plea, consider this,
That, in the course of justice, none of us
Should see salvation: we do pray for mercy;
And that same prayer doth teach us all to render
The deeds of mercy...."

Shylock has justice on his side (as we are assuming for now that the conservative does). However, there is something else to humanity. Even in the best case scenario for the conservative, there is an unmitigated Shylockian demand for justice, for rendering what one deserves regardless of the suffering caused by that demand.

That is not the way the liberal sees human life. As Portia says 'Mercy cannot be forced', cannot be required by law. But mercy is a moral virtue absent from the conservatives' narrow repertoire, from their view of life.

The traditional conservative loves the Ant and dislikes the Grasshopper and probably believes the entire fable is an expression of the way things are. The contemporary conservative probably has less love for the Ant, but her or his attitude toward the Grasshopper has degenerated from disliking to despising.

However their entire picture of the world, of life, of work, of judgment of our fellow human beings is mistaken on all counts.

SYMPOSIUM ON SYRIA (Issue #20)

With Andy Winnick, David M. Winnick, Ivan Light and Chris Rubel

In view of the importance of the issue concerning a U.S. punitive strike against Syria, **Progressive Democracy** *is publishing three different, and opposing, pieces on what we as liberals think should be done. They are very powerfully presented and argued. The Winnicks and Ivan Light have read each other's paper and respond to the contrary arguments. Rubel's essay is by someone not* *usually involved in these public discussions. Probably nowhere else than here can one get such a thorough and well-done review of the arguments by liberals for and against the U.S. striking at Syrian facilities.*

I.   Syria and the Principle of the Responsibility to Protect: The Moral, Strategic and Political-Economic Issues Involved In Determining the Appropriate Role of the U.S.

By Andy Winnick and David M. Winnick

America is in the midst of a debate about what its responsibility is with regard to Syria -- in particular: what should the U.S. do following the large-scale chemical weapons incident on August 21st if Syria does not abide by the agreement reached between the U.S. and Russia? But we think that much of this debate is focused on the wrong issues. There are critical moral questions involved, as well as vital political-economic issues that must be discussed.

A key issue is the principle of the Responsibility to Protect (R2P)

In 2005, after almost five years of meetings and reports following what happened in Rwanda, the United Nations, at a World Summit, adopted the principle of R2P in its final Outcomes Document. The Responsibility to Protect has three "pillars":

1. A state has a responsibility to protect its population from genocide, war crimes, crimes against humanity, and ethnic cleansing.
2. The international community has a responsibility to assist the state to fulfill its primary responsibility in this regard.
3. If the state manifestly fails to protect its citizens from the four mass atrocities mentioned in point #1 and if peaceful measures have failed, the international community has the responsibility to intervene through coercive measures such as economic sanctions, and, as a last resort, military intervention to protect the citizens who are being abused. Timeliness is a critical factor in deciding upon the required course of action.

In April, 2006, the Security Council formally reaffirmed these principles in resolution 1674. Then in January 2009, the UN Secretary General issued a report entitled *Implementing the Responsibility to Protect.*

To further understand the principle of the Responsibility to Protect, consider the question: What is the purpose of government? There should be, we hope, near-universal agreement that a government's most fundamental and basic responsibility is to ensure the safety and well-being of its citizens. All other responsibilities are secondary to, or a component of, the Responsibility to Protect the people it governs. This is the most sacred and important compact between a people and its government. It is no accident that

America's Founding Fathers began with the famous phrase with "**life**, liberty and the pursuit of happiness. "

Every government has this Responsibility to Protect its people. Any time a government is not in a position to ensure the safety and well-being of its people, it is obliged by logic and morality to request assistance. This applies in cases of natural disasters and invasions, for example. Likewise, it is the responsibility of all other governments to offer assistance proactively should they be in a position to help.

The corollary is that any time a government actively reneges on this fundamental responsibility and begins instead to kill the very people it is beholden to protect, that government has effectively abdicated its role as Protector of the People and has forfeited the right to govern and be recognized as officially representing that nation. Furthermore, since the use of violence against civilian populations for the purpose of furthering political goals is the very definition of terrorism, any government that systematically kills its own civilians is *de facto* a terrorist organization.

When such a government so completely fails to adhere to the Responsibility to Protect, then that responsibility must fall to the rest of the world's governments to actively step in on behalf of protecting the civilians being slaughtered. This is the key element in the U.N.'s statements on the Responsibility to Protect. Logically, the obligations of other nations vary according to each government's ability to intercede.

The strongest, richest and most powerful governments should clearly have the most responsibility simply because they can help the most.

Not only would not intervening send a clear message to the rogue government that it has *carte blanche* to continue, but it sends the same message to other governments that they can get away with such actions. In addition, any government that is in a position to act that actively decides not to act to prevent a slaughter has implicitly accepted the killing that will then take place and bears a significant responsibility for those deaths that occur.

However, there has always been a fatal flaw in the U.N.'s process for implementing the principle of the Responsibility to Protect: namely, that all coercive actions, including the use of military force, require a decision by the Security Council. There is no formal legal mechanism in existence for situations where coercion or intervention is clearly called for, but one or two permanent members of the Security Council vetoes any coercive actions, economic or military, to stop a state government from committing these crimes against its own people.

The fatal flaw in implementing the U.N's Responsibility to Protect, that is, the dependency upon the will of the U.N. Security Council, is all too evident in Syria. Russia and China have been determined to protect the Assad government in Syria, and have refused to allow any coercive action, economic or military, by the Security Council under R2P. And it appears that will continue even about the limited issue of chemical weapons.

Chemical weapons are not the key issue

In Syria, there have been over 100,000 people killed in the last two years, and currently more than 5,000 people are being killed every month. According to all reports, the vast majority of these are civilians who are being killed by the Assad government's forces in aerial bombings, attacks by helicopter gunships, attacks on cities by artillery, tanks and missiles, napalm bombs on a school, and, as of last count, 14 chemical attacks on neighborhoods in cities, most recently on August 21. Yes, the rebels have killed many as well, but not remotely on the same scale. Nevertheless, all the killing has to stop. Thus, while we agree that the use of chemical weapons is illegal under international law and that it is a horror that the world formally outlawed years ago, the key issue is not the 1400 or so killed on August 21, but the 100,000 killed so far, and the 5,000 per month being killed now. This is the morally compelling issue that must be addressed – how to end not simply the use of chemical weapons, but how to stop, or at least significantly reduce, the mass killings, and how to help forge a negotiated solution.

Let us be clear, even if, because of the specific threat of military action by the U.S., and because Russia finds it in its own best interests to get the chemical weapons out of Syria (in case Assad were to fall and the weapons fell into the "wrong" hands that might use them against Russia), all of the chemical weapons were to be secured or destroyed, the killing would go on. In fact, it has intensified in recent days despite the negotiations about chemical weapons.

The Role of the U.S. in the face of the U.N.'s failure to enforce the Responsibility to Protect

The only way to end the mass slaughter is if the U.S., and whatever allies it can muster, makes clear a <u>willingness</u> to destroy the Syrian government's military planes and helicopters, its tanks, artillery and missiles, if Assad does not agree to enter negotiations to end the civil war and accept a cease fire. This threat must be issued, not to win the war for the opponents of Assad, but to force him to agree to negotiations. At the same time, the U.S. should make it clear that as soon as Assad accepts these conditions and calls a cease fire, the U.S. will pledge to do everything it can to halt the flow of weapons to the rebels. It should then make it clear to the rebel forces that it will not support their continued attacks and that they too must agree to enter negotiations. If Assad does not stop the attacks on civilians, then the U.S. should move ahead to mount a serious, but short (a few days to one or two weeks) strike against Assad's weapons (not against civilian areas), and then make it clear the U.S. will mount further attacks if the Syrian government does not stop the attacks and negotiate. At the same time, the U.S. must put all possible pressure on those supplying weapons to the rebels to stop doing so and try to convince the opposition forces not to use the U.S.'s attacks as an excuse to escalate their own military efforts.

Why should the U.S. assume the role of enforcing R2P or, perhaps more to the point, what are the answers to the arguments being made that the U.S. should not take on this task, should not act as a World Policeman?

Let us try to identify the arguments being made that the U.S. should not unilaterally take on this role, should not even threaten military action, even if that is allowed for in the R2P, but such action is blocked in the Security Council. And in that context, we will argue why it should move to enforce R2P, unilaterally if necessary.

The U.S. has committed or contributed to many atrocities in the past.

These include the use of the Atom bomb against Japan, enabling Iraq to use chemical weapons against Iran, the use of Agent Orange in Vietnam, going to war in Iraq based upon lies about WMD, etc., etc. This is all true and horrible -- and is also irrelevant. The fact that the U.S. has committed atrocities in the past is not an argument against stopping another atrocity now. Is there some hypocrisy, some inconsistency involved in the U.S. currently acting in such a manner in Syria? Yes, but consistency is not the defining principle of foreign policy for any country and should not now be used to manipulate the U.S. into standing by while tens of thousands of civilians are slaughtered.

It needs to be kept in mind that the U.S. also has a history of militarily intervening to successfully save lives and end wars. The best examples are Bosnia, Kosovo and Libya, and the no-fly zone we imposed over northern Iraq in the early 1990's to protect the population there.

Will not a military attack against Syria mean more killing? How can we justify killing to stop other killing?

Here the answer is one of proportionality and targets. The U.S. should target military sites to eliminate planes, helicopters, missile launchers, artillery, tanks – not civilian areas. Would some civilians be killed? In all likelihood, yes, but hardly as many as are killed in a matter of days by the Syrian government's continuing use of these weapons. The U.S. would not bomb chemical weapons storage sites – that is indeed too dangerous, but it should target not just the delivery systems for those weapons, but also the other weapons that are killing thousands of civilians a month.

Is not the U.S. likely to get bogged down in another long war, as it did in Iraq and Afghanistan?

The answer is simply no. The U.S. did not get bogged down in Bosnia or Kosovo or Libya, or even in Iraq following Gulf War I. France is not bogged down in Mali. There is no reason to think that the U.S. would get bogged down in Syria following a short, but probably intense, attack on their military hardware.

Are there not likely to be retaliatory actions taken by Syria and its allies after an attack by the U.S.?

Large scale military attacks on the U.S. or its

allies are very unlikely due to a lack of capacity and due to other conflicting interests important to these actors. Everyone will need to stay alert, but this is not a significant threat. Are there likely to be some terrorist attacks mounted against U.S. interests? Here the answer is yes, some terrorist attacks are likely and have to be prepared for, especially against U.S. embassies and consulates. But again, the issue is one of proportionality. This is a risk the U.S. should take, morally and strategically, to save thousands of lives and enforce R2P.

The U.S. has just spent more than 3 trillion dollars in Iraq and Afghanistan.

The Military-Industrial-Congressional complex that Eisenhower warned us against remains powerful and already consumes too much of our money and resources, while far too little is being spent on education, job training, infrastructure, the stimulation of economic growth and the fight against growing income inequality. So how can one justify spending any more money in the Middle East on any military intervention there? The answer is twofold – the cost of short-term missile and air strikes against military targets in Syria is, relatively-speaking, a drop in the bucket – and the savings made by not doing this would simply go to other military activities. Does anyone seriously think that one penny of extra money will be spent on education, job training, infrastructure and the rest if the U.S. does not act in Syria? Does anyone seriously think that if the U.S. does mount such a limited action, Congress will use that as the basis to cut such civilian programs to a greater extent than they already do even if such action is not taken? We think not. The economic argument against action to support R2P has little content or relevance.

If the U.S. acts to enforce the Responsibility to Protect without U.N. Security Council authorization would this not mean that it would be violating international law, since the U.S. is not being directly threatened? If the U.S. adopt this policy is it not assuming to itself the role of World Policemen that should belong to the U.N.?

Yes, technically the U.S. would be acting outside the formal structure of international law. On the other hand, the U.S. has serious economic, political and other concerns that are being threatened by the millions of refugees that are presently destabilizing Turkey, Jordan, Lebanon, and even Iraq. Had the U.S., along with allies, years ago established safe heavens and no-fly zones inside Syria along its borders with these neighboring nations, much of this destabilization which so threatens our nation's interests could have been avoided. But this did not occur, and now it is too late for those then sensible options. So, we would argue that given the U.S.'s national interests and given the structural weakness in the U.N. with its veto powers in the Security Council and the lack of any mechanism for the General Assembly to overrule such a veto, the U.S. has a strong and moral right to act to enforce the Responsibility to Protect in the interests of not just the

Syrian people, but also to send a strong message to other governments tempted to follow Assad's path.

Does this mean we are urging that the U.S. presumes to act as the World's Policemen? With regard to enforcing the Right to Protect, the answer again is yes. Why should the U.S. assume this role? Part of the answer is simply because it can, it has the capacity, and because no one else currently has that ability. Hopefully, the U.S. will be able to share that responsibility with other nations, perhaps with a changing array of other nations depending upon the situation. And there well may be circumstances where it is not feasible for even the U.S. to do so. But nevertheless it is sadly true that because of the flaws in the decision-making structures of the U.N., there is often going to be no other alternative to the U.S. enforcing R2P. As many have said, not to decide is to decide. When good people refuse to act, evil dominates and controls. If there is no police, chaos is likely to rule. Let's act now when we can and morally should, while at the same time beginning an earnest attempt to strengthen the decision-making structures within the United Nations.

To summarize our recommendations:
We propose that the U.S. works closely with Russia, with allies, and with the U.N. to secure and destroy the chemical weapons in Syria, through peaceful means if possible. We also propose that the U.S. works with these same actors to try to move to a

cease-fire and to a peace conference to secure an end to the civil war and the transition to a new government under new leadership. But if the Syrian government does not comply regarding its chemical weapons, or even if it does, but then goes on using other more conventional weapons to kill yet thousands more of its civilians, then the U.S. should announce that it will proceed in the near term with an aerial attack on Syria's military weapons systems. If the killing does not stop, then that threat should be carried out.

At the same time, the U.S. should make clear that the intent is to force the Assad government into negotiations, not to defeat it militarily. In that spirit, it should also inform the opposition forces that the U.S. expects them to also accede to a cease-fire and to pursue serious negotiations. To this end, the U.S. must make clear the intent to block the supply of military weapons to the opposition if they refuse to cooperate. To weaken Assad, while arming the rebels, is to encourage the ascension to power of forces which may be no more desirable than Assad and which may lead to genocides of another sort. This is not an acceptable course of action for the U.S. As much as some may deplore this strategy or find it contradictory, the U.S. must use the threat of military force, and if necessary use such force, to end this civil war and the mass slaughter of the Syrian people.

Finally, the U.S. needs to mount a serious effort to work with other nations to strengthen the decision-making structures of the United Nations, so that the world can rely upon it, not the U.S., to authorize and implement enforcement of the Responsibility to Protect. For example, the U.S. could call for the General Assembly, by a two-thirds vote, to have the power to overrule a veto. This will require a long-term commitment to a diplomatic effort, with no guarantee of success. The world would quickly see whether even the U.S. is willing to allow for an override of a veto, even its own. But we argue that this is an effort we, the people must seriously mount, at least in the instance of implementing the Responsibility to Protect to block mass killings of civilians.

A Postscript Regarding the Chemical Weapons Issue

According to the most reliable sources we can find, we believe the following sequence of events has occurred. There were credible reports of the Syrian government's use of chemical weapons two months <u>before</u> Obama made his initial redline statement. It then took him those two months before speaking out with his redline statement to try to prevent further (not the first) use of these weapons. Assad then tested Obama's will by continuing with as many as ten more chemical attacks, some of greater intensity than the first, and observed that Obama's reaction was merely to complain and promise to arm the rebels. But then Obama did not send arms at all, instead he clandestinely had the CIA pull about 50 rebel fighters out of Syria to train and arm that small, almost insignificant force, to then have it be infiltrated back into Syria. Assad felt so emboldened and so safe from any serious countermove by Obama that he then went ahead with the August 21st attack. Only after Obama finally threatened military action did Assad even consider giving up his chemical weapons. The point is that had Obama made the threat the second time Assad used chemical weapons, it is almost certain that the later attacks would not have occurred. Thus the U.S. government bears significant culpability for the attack of August 21st.

Moreover, the move to have Assad give up his chemical weapons, did not, in fact, begin with Kerry's off-the-cuff remark at a U.K. press conference in early September. It began with conversations between Obama and Putin two years earlier, taken up by the two men again after August 21st and before Kerry's statement. The idea of Russia and the U.S. pushing Assad toward this was reported in non-U.S. media for weeks. Assad finally agreed only because of (i) the threat of U.S. attacks and (ii) pressure brought to bear by Russia. Why had Russia been floating this idea for the last two years? Because they are afraid that if Assad's government falls, a more extremist Islamist government might take over, and the chemical weapons could become aimed at Russia, especially because of the anger felt by the opposition due to Russia's support of Assad. Also, it was/is in Russia's interest to prevent a U.S. led attack on Assad's forces, not merely because they do not want to see those forces weakened, but also because from a global, strategic perspective, they do not want to see the U.S. extend its influence as it did in Bosnia, Kosovo, Libya and elsewhere.

But the essential point is that neither Russia nor Syria would have agreed to control and perhaps destroy Assad's chemical weapons now and on what seems to be an accelerated schedule, if the U.S did not make a credible threat to use military force. So those who are so pleased that these chemical weapons may be brought under international control via a peaceful process, and that those initial negotiations might even lead to some tentative moves toward a broader peace negotiation process, should understand that without the credible threat of military force none of this would have any chance of happening. If the U.S., now or in the near future, foreswears the use of military force, the possibility of a negotiated settlement immediately ends. This is especially true if Assad keeps his other weapons and the U.S. sits quietly by while thousands more are killed, while little is done to arm the rebels. In the future, if the U.S. commits to not using force and to simply waiting for action in the U.N., then the world will suffer a far worse fate than if we retain the option of selectively using military force in special circumstances when the Responsibility to Protect becomes germane. Does this raise the possibility of dangerous and inappropriate situations arising, like Iraq – yes. So we do indeed have to be very vigilant about when we, the people, allow consideration of the use of limited, focused, military action to enforce the Responsibility to Protect. But the alternative to such a situational approach is even more dangerous.

II. Don't Attack Syria

By Ivan Light

Several prominent Democrats came out early in support of Obama's projected airstrikes against Syria. With all due respect to them, sorry, I oppose their war policy. Of course, we are all hoping, without exception, that Russian/American cooperation will permit a diplomatic solution to this world crisis. But, what if it does not? Should the US then proceed to attack Syria as Obama and Kerry have threatened? Andrew Winnick thinks our UN requires the United States to do so. He cites a 2005 UN resolution that creates a member state "responsibility to protect" vulnerable people against genocide, war crimes, human rights violations, etc. Please note. The UN resolution assigns this responsibility to the "international community," not to the United States. If the international community would step up to the plate for Syria, I would have no objection to US co-participation. The world needs a stronger United Nations.

Unfortunately, with the possible exception of France, the rest of the world shows no interest in joining our punitive attack on Syria. Britain has rejected it. We will be alone again with a rag-tag-and-bobtail collection of small, client countries that send token support. What would then have occurred is another assignment to the United States of full responsibility for an illegal, punitive war, as well as exclusive responsibility for the consequences of such an attack whether they include a larger war in the Middle East, another unforeseen trillion dollar war bill, or both. Either the US takes unilateral action – or nothing is done. In this case, everyone's business has become the responsibility of the United States alone.

The reason the US is assigned this exclusive responsibility, Dr. Winnick correctly observes, is that only the US has the capability to undertake the role of world policeman, which he candidly acknowledges we now play. We must because "we can." Of course, "we can" because the US spends almost as much as the rest of the world combined on military power, and also spends half of our tax dollars on the same military capability. This capability arises in turn because the US has been the world's policeman in the past half century, fighting many useless and unnecessary wars at our own expense in blood and treasure. The rest of the world has learned to sit back and let the Americans undertake this role while they do nothing. We must because we can; we can because we became world policemen back in 1947, and we have been carrying the torch ever since. So now we have to do it again. This is what our leadership wants us to believe.

But it is not 1947 any longer. In 1947, the US was a lonely world powerhouse because all the other big countries had been ruined by the Second World War, their human resources and infrastructures laid waste. Eighty percent of the world's gold was in Fort Knox, Ky. But this is no longer the case. Since 1947, other countries have wisely taken advantage of the US military umbrella to build up their civilian infrastructure, including educational systems, railroads, harbors, medical care, bridges, highways, housing, airports, parks, and public transit while the US has allowed its infrastructure to deteriorate in order to free resources for policing the world. Our economic infrastructure is now in a shambles as a result of this protracted and ultimately prodigal policy of global military interventions backed by disproportionate military spending.

Consider the logic of those who demand that the US intervene in Syria on the side of the rebels. The US has played world policeman in the past; therefore, the US is the only power capable of undertaking it today. Therefore, the US must continue to do so today! No matter that the US is still paying for misguided and counter-productive wars in Iraq and Afghanistan that have already cost us three trillion dollars as well as thousands of human lives. World policeman is still an exclusively American responsibility.

"To everything there is a season." There was a season to play the role of world policeman, and now there is a season to tell the community of nations that the US is prepared to assume its fair share of global military burdens, but no more. This is that season. It is time now for other nations to step up to the plate, and assume their fair share of the burden of preserving peace and preventing genocide. Unfortunately, the other nations will not assume this responsibility until and unless they learn that the United States will no longer do so in their absence. Why should they? They will "ride free" as long as Uncle Sam pays their fare. True, renunciation of the role of world policeman is a big step; and it will usher in a multi-polar world more similar to 1930 than to 1947. Germany will rearm; so will Japan. Brazil, China, India, and Indonesia will arm. But there really is no realistic alternative to a multi-polar world now, and a strengthened United Nations is the appropriate remedy, not a bankrupt, drained, prostrate, and ruined United States. This transition to a stronger United Nations has to start someday. If not now, when? The present moment is a splendid time to begin the transition to this next phase of world history.

There are other constraints, of course, although I personally think that the biggest is renunciation of the role of world policeman that the US assumed after World War II. Attacking Syria would violate international law, involving the creation of yet another "coalition of the willing" as a fig leaf for unilateral US action. John Kerry says that "civilization" depends on violating international law in this way. I think that cliché was introduced to American political discourse during the "rape of Belgium" in 1914, and then justified the "war to end wars." If you recall, the First World War did not end wars; it begat the Second World War, which begat the Cold War, which begat so many other wars, including now the Syrian civil war. The "defense of civilization" has now become so trite and tired a call to arms that it amazes me the politicians still offer it, and think that Americans will flock to the colors on hearing it. "Fool me once, shame on you; fool me twice, shame on me."

John Kerry says that "this is not the time" to change diplomatic direction. According to John Kerry, Americans must continue to play the role of world policeman at least one more time. The drunk says "this is not the time" to stop drinking; please give me one more drink. The smoker says "this is not the time" to quit smoking; please let me have one more cigarette. Our political *status quo* is begging for another military fix. "Please give us just one more little war in the Middle East. Then we'll stop playing world policeman." Fat chance. In fact, this is the *ideal time* to challenge the military-industrial-Congressional complex that is leading our nation to ruin. For the first time since the mid-1970s, the American people have them on the run. This is the perfect time to repudiate the military-industrial-Congressional lobby that, unlike Syria, really does threaten our country's welfare and future.

John Kerry says the air attack on Syria is in the US national interest. I agree that our national interest is a valid and important policy template. I can also see that embarrassing Obama in front of the world would not be in the interest of the Obama administration, including

John Kerry. But the political interest and reputation of the Obama administration is not the same as the long-term US national interest although Obama's spokespeople duplicitously seek to conflate the two just as, dare I say it, so did the spokespeople of George W. Bush. If the US should stop being the self-appointed global policeman, should cut military spending back to European levels, and should just become a member in good standing of the community of nations, wouldn't that represent the pursuit of our long-term national interest? Political embarrassment to the Obama administration and to Secretary Kerry is of slight consequence relative to that long-term interest of the American people.

Everyone must answer these questions. Isn't the diversion of our tax money to world policing undermining the our civilian economy, wrecking our schools, impoverishing our people, discouraging green investment by the government, diffusing militarism in our society, and turning our country into a national security state? Won't these hateful trends continue and intensify as long as the military-industrial-Congressional complex imposes its warlike foreign policies?

In reply to and defiance of the overwhelmingly negative messages from her constituents, who overwhelmingly oppose the drift to war in Syria, Senator Diane Feinstein objects, that the US must intervene on its own to strip the chemical weapons from Syria's brutal military dictatorship on strictly

215

humanitarian grounds. Assuming that is so, for the sake of argument, is attacking Syria really, as Dr. Winnick also proposes, the "only way" to deal with the Assad regime? How about international and diplomatic pressures and sanctions such as were directed at Iraq, but discontinued prematurely in the interest of launching an ill-advised war? What about undertaking financial support of the refugees in concert with other countries, and encouraging them to leave Syria for neighboring states? This policy would move the refugees out of the war zone, leaving the contending parties to fight their contest to a finish. Finally, what about offering to exchange Assad's chemical weapons cache at its fair market value for conventional weapons, including napalm, white phosphorus, and Agent Orange, and extending the same offer to the rebels? This policy might obtain all the chemical weapons at a price well below what a war would cost and without bloodshed. Other humane, civilized, and rich countries could volunteer to defray the cost by exchanging poison gas for conventional weapons from their stockpiles.

We must consider as well the possibility that stripping Assad of chemical weapons would leave these weapons exclusively in the hands of Syria's rebels. President Putin of Russia maintains that rebels also used poison gas on 14 occasions, and the UN has just begun to investigate the charge. Should that charge prove true, premature military intervention could tilt the battlefield balance in Syria toward the rebels, enabling their victory. Who are these rebels? Few are democrats. Most are Sunni Moslems determined to resolve a religious dispute with Shia Moslems and Alawite Moslems by killing them. A large component is foreign (non-Syrian) jihadists sympathetic with the terrorists who attacked us on Nine Eleven. Among these, the Al-Nusra Front consists entirely of Al-Queda fanatics, considered the most radical and dangerous of all the jihadists. Should the Al–Nusra Front prevail, they might initiate a retaliatory bloodbath against Muslim heretics (the Shia and Alawite), and the substantial Christian minority in Syria. Then the United States would confront another humanitarian disaster inviting military intervention.

We should not forget the lessons of the past. The US armed Afghan jihadists against the Soviet Union; later the victorious jihadists turned their weapons against us. This could happen again when the United States intervenes once again in Syria to protect the Christian minority from persecution by the rebels. It is stupid enough to impoverish your own country in thankless and counter-productive wars abroad; it is even stupider to do so in support of fanatical enemies.

"Hell no, we won't go" still seems about right.

III. Assad is in Charge Even Here

By Chris Rubel

Assad used chemical weapons to do more efficiently what guns and bombs don't do. He has effectively pushed Obama and the recalcitrant, anti-Obama Senate and House free-loaders deeper into a divide. Obama played the hand of a leader, declaring a Red Line, thereby declaring himself the leader he would hope to be and has the right to be. But Assad, and his kin, can sit back and be entertained by the drama he and/or they triggered.

We have the wisdom and the assurance we will not use our worn-out military "boots on the ground" to escalate our involvement in the chaos of the Middle East. But, we have an appetite always for using our technological devices whenever possible to show the world what free enterprise and brilliant weaponry can accomplish. Being the world's number one purveyor of weapons, using them is a major source of advertising. Maybe our missiles and drones can convince others we don't need constant and intense diplomacy, bargaining, building international coalitions to diminish the power of leaders who thrive on terror, creating victims in their sphere's of influence and genocide.

Some of the resistance Americans have to another possible battleground, another sponge to soak up our resources, our armaments, our fatigued military, is that we have not seen much at all that smells like victory or even a hint of democracy developing in Iraq or Afghanistan. Even Egypt, where we pour money and had hopes of a democratic government, is teetering on the brink of who knows what despite our bucks.

Could someone please list our military endeavors that have been victorious on our terms or any other terms? I'm a Korea Conflict veteran and I don't recall coming home from that one bursting my military buttons as a victor. I was in the Air Force and can take credit for helping to drop Napalm on thousands of civilians as the Truce Talks were taking shape. How about Vietnam? Does anyone remember Vietnam, besides those who came home to abuse and disdain after the dead, wounded, and the countless veterans with Agent Orange problems and nightmares the VA couldn't assuage? By the way, is someone more dead from chemical or nuclear (or, as George W. would have said, "nukular") weapons than from bullets, bayonets, phosphorous bombs, or flame throwers?

Leave it to war-weary civilians and military to ask such elementary questions as the following:

1) What specific targets will we strike that will not involve innocent people and possibly explode the very chemical weapons we are so against, even if we might have provided these weapons?

There are rumors nourished by those who cherish rumors that the very weapons that Assad used are some of those that Saddam hid from us, sending them to Syria before we could find them. Who knows? I don't.

2) What is our strategy if Syria decides to escalate the odds by striking Israel? With Israel's military ready machine and the certain involvement of the U. S., Syria's striking Israel in retaliation would be the match to light up the Middle East war for sure, bringing in Iran, and,

219

perhaps, Russia.

3) What happens if Putin decides to throw his chips in with Assad, throwing high tech stuff back at our installations, ships in the area, our oil supplies there, etc.? Add to this China and what will China do, or, for that matter Britain and France?

4) Do we have an idea of whom in the civil mix in Syria (and anywhere else for that matter) we want to end up being in charge, the approved-by-us government of a "new" Syria? We're not sure whoever will replace a fallen Assad, along with his mother and brother, is going to be any better, any less a source of conflict, atrocities, and terror.

5) Are we willing to initiate a new Selective Service call up, this time drafting everyone eligible and not relying on the current one percent of our population who are now the fodder for our military whims? Are you willing to see your sons, daughters, brothers, sisters, lovers, or even some of those teenaged taggers and wanna-be gang members with nothing to do, be called into the military?

6) Does anyone have any idea about the financial commitment this strike will yield? Does that matter?

7) Are politicians so eager to solve our economic problems that they will relish the possibility of increased military involvement, even, perhaps, a war in the Middle East?

8) This last one is because I'm getting too depressed to think up more to say on the subject.

9) Oh yes. One more thought. Do we have any

desire for the United Nations to work on the world's behalf? I guess this is getting off the subject. Maybe?

Assad holds the strings to this balloon and he and his court are riding around as respected leader(s), earning the praise and respect of much of the world; those who despise America already and would love to have a Middle East anybody give us the jitters and watch us flounder at their provocations. Besides, what is better than this dilemma to obscure the hot topics of immigration, defunding Obamacare, closing abortion clinics, etc., etc.? The media have grabbed the Syrian civil strife with relief, because our constant issues are losing an audience.

I guess the best I can do is to ventilate, which this piece might accomplish for me. If anyone has something to say or write about any aspect of the above, have at it. I know we're not lately in the habit of truly talking about controversy in public places, but perhaps we can begin to change that.

Here's an afterthought: How about sending all the money we'd spend on striking Syria's undefined targets to the refugee camps to provide medical, educational, and other services for those who might go on living after we would have made matters worse in Syria? How about doing that? What would it be like for America to be known as a world power that furthers anything humanitarian in nature? Would we lose anything if our military might dwindled to a defense status, giving way to improving conditions for the bereft masses here and there?

Government and Banking (Issue #4)

The relationship between the Federal Government and our banking system needs serious reform. Three changes are especially necessary.

America's present banking system has severe flaws. The biggest banks speculate with much of their assets. Despite holding trillions of dollars in assets, banks fail to lend and to rescue the economy by doing so; their fear of recession becomes a self-fulfilling prophecy. Meanwhile, the government must borrow from the Federal Reserve in order to stimulate the economy through deficit spending; as a result, we taxpayers incur a big debt to be repaid in the future (probably by our children and grandchildren). This newly created and spent money remains in the economic system, threatening to ignite inflation later. The Federal Reserve can lend to the government and to private banks, but it isn't authorized to lend to the Main Street economy, i.e., other businesses and consumers.

Here are some thoughts about reforming our banking system.

THE GOVERNMENT SHOULD BE A LENDER, NOT A BORROWER. Instead of borrowing money from the Federal Reserve, the government should be able to create money and lend it to businesses and consumers. This will stimulate the economy during recessions but avoid creating a huge national debt. The debt will be owed by the borrowers to the government, not by the government and ultimately by the taxpayers. As the economy improves and the loans are repaid, the created money will disappear, acting as a brake on asset bubbles and price inflation.

THE GOVERNMENT NEEDS A REAL NATIONAL BANK. Most Americans don't know it, but the Federal Reserve is owned by a consortium of private banks, which elect most of the Federal Reserve Board, although the President selects the Chair and Vice-Chair. Through the Fed, these private banks create money and lend it to the government by purchasing Treasury bonds. They, not the government and taxpayers, receive the profits from that lending. To carry out the strategy described in item #1 above, the government needs to be its own bank, not a borrower from the Federal Reserve. The closest thing to a real national bank in the U.S. is the state bank of North Dakota. It partners with private banks to promote economic activity within North Dakota, and it pays its profits to the state government. This has enabled North Dakota to have the lowest unemployment rate in the U.S. and to have a balanced budget every year.

See: http://www.alternet.org/story/152285/north_dakota_fig
_wall_street%27s_influence_with_a_state_bank_/?page=1

PRIVATE BANKS SHOULD LEND, NOT SPECULATE. Small community banks mainly lend to businesses and consumers in their area. Credit unions lend to their members. This lending is the purpose and social justification for banking. Big banks, however, devote much of their capital to speculation, which makes them and their key employees extremely wealthy when it succeeds but threatens the existence of the banks when it fails. A financial corporation should have to choose between being a speculation machine and a bank. If it chooses to speculate, government insurance should not protect its investors. A federally insured bank should be limited to lending. This will encourage investors and savers to place their money with real banks that support the real economy and will relieve taxpayers of the obligation to bail out unsuccessful speculators.

Reforms such as these would promote economic activity, stimulate the economy when it's weak, restrain it when it's in danger of overheating, avoid burdening present and future generations of taxpayers with debt, and lessen the likelihood of future economic crises such as that which caused our Great Recession.

Has Racism Really Vanished? (Issue #22)
By Charles Bayer

Of course not. Going underground is not vanishing. Anyone who sincerely believes that white male opposition to Obama has nothing to do with race is thoroughly naïve.

I would like to believe that racism in America is only a long-gone sad episode in our national history, and that we are at last free of its shame. I am here not referring to some generic definition of racism, but to the racial bigotry that began with the coming of slavery and is still focused on African Americans. Certainly, to a large extent we have become colorblind. And yet I believe there are still deeply imbedded pustules of racial prejudice that continue to affect attitudes and habits.

Instead of waiting until the end of this column, let me state my conclusion up front. I believe much of the hostility that has plagued President Obama is the result of a lingering racial prejudice. There are still pockets of bigotry that cannot accept a Black President and certain sectors of the Republican Party have taken advantage of this bitterness. It comes wrapped in different code names, but I'll get to that shortly.

225

First, a bit of American history. Following the Civil War and Reconstruction, bigotry basically remained the governing philosophy of the Democratic Party in the South. The former Confederacy was firmly lodged in Democratic hands. This party was the home of the Klan, the White Citizens Councils, and Jim Crow. The worst public bigots were US Senators from those States. The "Solid (Democratic) South" dissolved with the passage of a Civil Rights plank in the 1948 Democratic platform, followed by Lyndon Johnson's Civil Rights and Voting Rights Acts of 1964 and 1965. The Dixiecrats, under Strom Thurmond, disavowed their Democratic roots and bitterly fought their former party and its northern and western blocs.

Richard Nixon realized that these disaffected Democrats might be easy pickings, and developed what became known as "the Southern Strategy." Its fundamental plan was to capitalize on the lingering bigotry against African Americans and the plan succeeded: the Republicans won victories in five of the formerly solid Democratic states in 1964 and 1968. The profoundly prejudiced Strom Thurmond delivered the Dixiecrats to his new political allegiance, and led the fight to stall integration, which was sweeping much of the nation.

The Republican political wizard, Kevin Phillips, put it this way, "The more Negroes vote as democrats (sic) in the South, the sooner the Negrophobic whites will become Republicans." "States' Rights" became a code word for opposition to civil rights legislation.

As far back at 1954, Lee Atwater, another Republican operative, opined, "You can't say nigger—that hurts you, backfires—so you say things like forced busing, states rights ... This is much more abstract."

Having lost the argument about voting rights for African Americans, in more recent years these same now solidly Republican state governments have sought to redesign their congressional districts in order to minimize black votes, which tended to go heavily Democratic.

"Stand your ground" is still another coded way to control what many white people think is the criminal mind of their African American neighbors. Trayvon Martin didn't just happen to be African American, he was stalked because he was.

The vicious attack on the nutrition vouchers formerly called "food stamps," is not so quietly aimed at so-called welfare mothers, who are falsely assumed to be largely Black.

The Robertsons' "Duck Dynasty" racism may not be the norm in their part of the world, but it is not an isolated example of what goes on when nobody outside is listening.

Affirmative Action, which gave African Americans a way to make up for continued lost opportunities, inferior separate and unequal schools, blighted neighborhoods and invasive poverty, is being attacked in the conservative press and now in the courts. So you hear stories about how some deserving white person was denied admission to a university even through her/his academic record was better than that of an African American who was admitted, as if that is now the essence of racism.

And to top it off, the Supreme Court has effectively dismantled the Voting Rights Act by holding that its enforcement is no longer necessary.

Racism in America has not disappeared, it has simply gone underground. Anyone who really believes that among working-class white males President Obama's color is not an issue is either naive or simply denying a political reality. The good news is that the United States is becoming less dominated by white males every year. Latinos, Asians and African Americans are increasingly a formidable political force. As long as red states fail to come to terms with this reality, they will lose political ground. That is just the way the arc of justice continues to bend.

Inheritance Taxes: The Conservative Contradiction (Issue #14)

By Merrill Ring

The Progressive/Liberal and the Conservative have very different views as to 'death duties' – the Conservative should in principle demand that a received estate should be taxed away, the Progressive is much more supportive of family values.

Sometimes it is called an estate tax, sometimes an inheritance tax - 'death duty' is the misleading and informal name. It should make a difference which of those names is attached to the tax, though in practice (around the world so far as I can see) one or the other name is used without any thought given to the matter.

Now while market liberals (neo-liberals) think there should be no taxes or perhaps some very small taxation to support no more than 'the night-watchman state', that particular form of taxation with the two names is high on their list of condemned forms of taxation. Yet the principles by which they condemn it are contradictory.

First, as to the names. To call something an 'estate tax' would be to conceive of it as a tax levied on a person's resources when he or she dies and before the resources are passed on to a later generation. On the other hand, an inheritance tax would be a tax to be paid by the inheritor on the resources they have acquired by inheriting them. The question of the appropriate name is relevant to the issue of what the point of the tax is.

Now the conservative will say that the person whose estate it is has the right to dispose of it as they see fit. Supposing that the resources - money, land, whatever - have been legitimately acquired (at least by normal social understanding of what is legitimate), then they are the person's property, having been acquired by the person's own effort, by the so-called sweat of their brow (a large mis-description), through his/her work. Then, the conservatives say, that person has the right to dispose of what is theirs as they wish and no one else, certainly not the state, has the right to interfere.

The problem in the conservative view, what they overlook in insisting upon the freedom to dispose of one's resources, is not with the disposal but with their receipt by the heir. Have the resources been acquired by the inheritor by their own effort, by the sweat of their brow, by their work? Overwhelmingly the answer is No – in the standard case such resources are received because the inheritors are the off-spring or other relatives of those who give. It is not a matter of work and receiving the fruits of one's labor – which is the standard conservative view of what rightly belongs to us individually. It is a matter of transmission to a family member of resources that he/she has not earned themselves from the sweat of their brow. Hence on the very principle that conservatives use to justify freedom to give the resources, the recipient does not warrant having them, is not justified in acquiring them.

A thoughtful and principled economic conservative would <u>demand</u> that there be a very large, if not complete tax on resources inherited. Each individual must possess resources only if they have engaged in work and earned the rewards of that effort. The older generation, thus, has the right to dispose of their property as they see fit – the younger generation, however, has no right to have it. Tax it away – support the night-watchman state from those resources.

But of course existing economic conservatives are not thoughtful and principled in this matter. They stand with the wealthy. They ignore their principles when it comes to matters of inheritance.

What should a progressive say about the tax? First, we should call it and think of it as a tax levied not on a person's estate at death but on the inheritor. However, since we do not have the same principles regarding work and what should rightfully belong to one, we do not have to think that a good inheritance tax would remove all or nearly all of what is inherited, leaving the younger generation to stand only upon their own two feet. We progressives are willing to give people a hand, an opportunity, as witnessed by progressive redistribution schemes. And families, not just individuals, are a part of our view of human life. Transferring some resources from one generation to the next is a humanly important way of giving people a hand while maintaining family structures.

But there are others in our society who deserve a better standard of living than has come to them by the contingencies of life. Consequently, an inheritance tax makes sense as a matter of redistribution. The problem for the progressive is to find the right level of inheritance taxation: one that does not maintain undesirable and undeserved inequality, but recognizes that it is right to help our children, as well as strangers, to achieve a decent life.

Note: in case you don't think that inherited

money plays an important role in giving people a head-start in economic life in this country, consult the recent report *Born on Third Base: What the Forbes 400 Really Says about Wealth & Opportunity in America* (from the non-profit United for a Fair Economy – see www.faireconomy.org) It takes $1.1 billion to make the top 400 this year. Twenty percent of those on the list simply inherited enough to make the list. Another twenty percent inherited not quite enough to make it and had to supplement the "sizeable asset" they inherited by some other means. Keeping it in the family, seventeen percent of the 400 had another family member on the list. Those are major signs of the dynastic wealth in this country.